AUTHOR'S INTRODUCTION

I have written this work not to teach people what they do not know, but to remind them of what they already know and is very evident to them. You will find in most of my words only things which most people know, and which they entertain no doubts. But to the extent that they are well known and their truths revealed to all, so is forgetfulness in relation to them extremely prevalent. The benefit to be obtained from this work is not derived from a single reading - it is possible that the reader will find that he has learned little after having read it that he did not know before. Its benefit is to be derived, rather, through review and persistent study, by which one is reminded of those things which, by nature, he is prone to forget and through which he is caused to take to heart the duty that he tends to overlook.

A consideration of the general state of affairs will show that most people of quick intelligence and keen mentality devote most of their thought and speculation to the subtleties of wisdom and the profundities of analysis, each according to the inclination of his intelligence and his natural bent. There are some who expend a great deal of effort in studying creation and nature. Others devote their thought to astronomy and mathematics. Others to the arts. There are those who go more deeply into sacred studies, into the study of the holy Torah, some occupying themselves with Halachic discussions, others with Midrash and others with legal decisions.

Few, however, who devote thought and study to perfection of Divine service - to love, fear, communion and all of the other aspects of saintliness. It is not that they consider this knowledge unessential; if questioned each one will keep that it is of paramount importance and that one who is not clearly versed in it cannot be deemed truly wise. Their failure to devote more attention to it stems rather from its being so manifest and so obvious to them that they see no need for spending much time upon it. Consequently, this study and the reading of works of this kind have been left to those of a not too sensitive, almost dull intelligence. These you will see immersed in the study of saintliness, not stirring from it. It has reached the stage that when one sees another engaging in saintly conduct, he cannot help but suspect him of dullwittedness. This state of affairs results in evil consequences both for those who possess wisdom and for those who do not, causing both classes to lack true saintliness, and rendering it extremely rare. The wise lack it because of their limited consideration of it and the unwise because of their limited grasp. The result is that saintliness is construed by most to consist in the recitation of many Tehillim, very long confessions, difficult fasts, and ablutions in ice and snow - all of which are incompatible with intellect and which reason cannot accept.

Truthful, desirable saintliness is far from being conceptualized by us, for it is obvious that a person does not concern himself with what does not occupy a place in his mind. And though the beginnings and foundations of saintliness are implanted in every person's heart, if he does not occupy himself with them, he will witness details of saintliness without recognizing them and he will trespass upon them without feeling or perceiving that he is doing so. For sentiments of saintliness, fear and love of Hashem, and purity of heart are not so deeply rooted within a person as to obviate the necessity of his employing certain devices in order to acquire them. In this respect they differ from natural states such as sleep and wakefulness, hunger and satiety, and all other reactions which are stamped in one's nature, in that various methods and devices are perforce required for their acquisition. There is also no lack of deterrents which keep saintliness at a distance from a person, but then again there is no lack of devices by which these deterrents may be held afar. How, then, is it conceivable that it not be necessary to expend a great deal of time upon this study in order to know these truths and the manner in which they may be acquired and fulfilled? How will this wisdom enter a person's heart if he will not seek it? And since every man of wisdom recognizes the need for perfection of Divine service and the necessity for its purity and cleanliness, without which it is certainly completely unacceptable, but repulsive and despised - "For Hashem searches all hearts and understands the inclination of all thoughts" (I Chronicles 28:9) - what will we answer in the day of reproof if we weaken in this study and forsake that which is so incumbent upon us as to be the very essence of what Hashem our G -d asks of us? Is it fitting that our intelligence exert itself and labor in speculations which are not binding upon us, in fruitless argumentation, in laws which have no application to us, while we leave to habit and abandon to mechanical observance our great debt to our Creator? If we do not look into and analyze the question of what constitutes true fear of Hashem and what its ramifications are, how will we acquire it and how will we escape wordly vanity which renders our hearts forgetful of it? Will it not be forgotten and go lost even though we recognize its necessity? Love of Hashem, too - if we do not make an effort to implant it in our hearts, utilizing all of the means which direct us toward it, how will it exist within us? Whence will enter into our souls intimacy with and ardor toward Hashem and toward His Torah if we do not give heart to His greatness and majesty which engender this intimacy in our hearts? How will our thoughts be purified if we do not strive to rescue them from the imperfections infused in them by physical nature? And all of the character traits, which are in such great need of correction and cultivation -who will cultivate and correct them if we do not give heart to them and subject them to exacting scrutiny? If we analyzed the matter honestly would we not extract the truth and thereby benefit ourselves, and also be of benefit to others by instructing them in it? As stated by Solomon (Mishlei 2:4), "If you seek it as silver and search for it as treasure, then you will understand the fear of Hashem." He does not say, "Then you will understand philosophy; then youwill understand astronomy; then you will understand medicine; then you will understand legal judgments and decisions." We see, then, that for fear of G -d to be understood, it must be sought as silver and searched for as treasure. All this is part of our heritage and is accepted in substance by every devout individual.

Again, is it conceivable that we should find time for all other branches of study and none for this study? Why should a man not at least set aside for himself certain times for this speculation if he is obliged in the remainder of his time to turn to other studies or undertakings? Scripture states (Job 28:28), "Hen fear of Hashem - this is wisdom." Chazal comment (Shabbath 31b), " `Hen' means `one,' for in Greek `one' is designated as `Hen' (Ev). " "We see, then, that fear, and only fear, is accounted wisdom. And there is no doubt that what entails no analysis is not considered wisdom. The truth is that all of these things require great analysis if they are to be known in truth and not through imagination and deceitful supposition. How much more so if they are to be acquired and attained. One who thinks into these matters will see that saintliness does not hinge upon those things which are put at a premium by the foolishly "saintly," but upon true perfection and great wisdom. This is what Moshe our Teacher, may Peace be upon him, teaches us in saying (Dvarim 10:12), "And now, Israel, what does Hashem ask of you, but that you fear Hashem to walk in all His ways, and to love Him and serve Hashem with all your heart and all your soul, to observe the mitzvos of Hashem and His statutes.." Here all the features of perfection of Divine service that are appropriate in relation to Hashem are included. They are: fear of Hashem, walking in His ways, love, wholeheartedness, and observance of the mitzvos.

"Fear of Hashem" denotes fear of the Majesty of Hashem, fearing Him as one would a great and mighty king, and being ashamed at one's every movement in consequence of His greatness, especially when speaking before Him in prayer or engaging in the study of His Torah.

"Walking in His ways" embodies the whole area of cultivation and correction of character traits. As Chazal have explained, "As He is merciful, be also merciful..." The essence of all this is that a person conform all of his traits and all the varieties of his actions to what is just and ethical. Chazal have thus summarized the idea (Avos 2.1): "All that is praiseworthy in its doer and brings praise to him from others;" that is, all that leads to the end of true good, namely, strengthening of Torah and furthering of brotherliness.

"Love" - that there be implanted in a person's heart a love for Hashem which will arouse his soul to do what is pleasing before Him, just as his heart is aroused to give pleasure to his father and mother. He will be grieved if he or others are lacking in this; he will be jealous for it and he will rejoice greatly in fulfilling aught of it. "Whole-heartedness" - that service before Hashem be characterized by purity of motive, that its end be His service alone and nothing else. Included in this is that one's heart be complete in Divine service, that his interests not be divided or his observance mechanical, but that his whole heart be devoted to it.

"Observance of all the mitzvos," as the words imply, is observance of the whole body of mitzvos with all of their fine points and conditions.

All of these principles require extensive interpretation. Chazal have categorized these elements in a different, more detailed formulation, in which they are arranged according to the order necessary for their proper acquisition. Their words are contained in a Baraitha mentioned in different places in the Talmud, one of them, the chapter "Before their festivals" (Avodah Zara 20b). From this R. Pinchas ben Yair adduced:

`Torah leads to Watchfulness; Watchfulness leads to Zeal; Zeal leads to Cleanliness; Cleanliness leads to Separation; Separation leads to Purity; Purity leads to Saintliness; Saintliness leads to Humility; Humility leads to Fear of Sin; Fear of Sin leads to Holiness; Holiness leads to the Holy Spirit, and the Holy Spirit leads to the Revival of the Dead."

It is on the basis of this Baraitha that I have undertaken to write this work, to teach myself and others of the conditions for perfect Divine service according to their gradations. In relation to each one, I shall explain its nature, its divisions or details, the manner of acquiring it, and its deterrents and the manner of guarding against them, so that I and all those who are pleased to do so may read it to learn to fear Hashem and not forget our duty before Him. That which the earthiness of nature seeks to remove from our hearts, reading and contemplation will summon to our consciousness, and will awaken us to what is incumbent upon us.

May Hashem be with our aspirations and keep our feet from stumbling, and may there be fulfilled in us the supplication of the Psalmist, beloved of his G- d (Tehillim 86:11), "Teach me, O Hashem, Your ways; I shall walk in Your truth. Make one my heart to fear Your Name." Amen, so may be His will.

CHAPTER I

CONCERNING MAN'S DUTY IN THE WORLD

THE FOUNDATION OF SAINTLINESS and the root of perfection in the service of Hashem lies in a man's coming to see clearly and to recognize as a truth the nature of his duty in the world and the end toward which he should direct his vision and his aspiration in all of his labors all the days of his life.

Chazal have taught us that man was created for the sole purpose of rejoicing in Hashem and deriving pleasure from the splendor of His Presence; for this is true joy and the greatest pleasure that can be found. The place where this joy may truly be derived is the World to Come, which was expressly created to provide for it; but the path to the object of our desires is this world, as Chazal have said (Avos 4:21), "This world is like a corridor to the World to Come."

The means which lead a man to this goal are the mitzvos, in relation to which we were commanded by Hashem. The place of the performance of the mitzvos is this world alone.

Therefore, man was placed in this world first - so that by these means, which were provided for him here, he would be able to reach the place which had been prepared for him, the World to Come, there to be sated with the goodness which he acquired through them. As Chazal have said (Eruvin 22a), "Today for the mitzvos' performance and tomorrow for receiving reward."

When you look further into the matter, you will see that only union with Hashem constitutes true perfection, as King David said (Tehillim 73:28), "But as for me, the nearness of Hashem is my good," and (Tehillim 27:4), "I asked one thing from Hashem; that will I seek - to dwell in Hashem's house all the days of my life..." For this alone is the true good, and anything besides this which people deem good is nothing but emptiness and deceptive worthlessness. For a man to attain this good, it is certainly fitting that he first labor and persevere in his exertions to acquire it. That is, he should persevere so as to unite himself with Hashem by means of actions which result in this end. These actions are the mitzvos.

Hashem has put man in a place where the factors which draw him away from Hashem are many. These are the earthy desires which, if he is pulled after them, cause him to be drawn further from and to depart from the true good. It is seen, then, that man is in a raging battle. For all the affairs of the world, whether for the good or for the bad, are trials to a man: Poverty on the one hand and wealth on the other, as Solomon said (Mishlei 30:9), "Lest I become satiated and deny, saying, `Who is Hashem?' or lest I become impoverished and steal..." Serenity on the one hand and suffering on the other; so that the battle rages against him to the fore and to the rear. If he is valorous, and victorious on all sides, he will be the "Whole Man," who will succeed in uniting himself with his Creator, and he will leave the corridor to enter into the Palace, to glow in the light of life. To the extent that he has subdued his evil inclination and his desires, and withdrawn from those factors which draw him further from the good, and exerted himself to become united with it, to that extent will he attain it and rejoice in it.

If you look more deeply into the matter, you will see that the world was created for man's use. In truth, man is the center of a great balance. For if he is pulled after the world and is drawn further from his Creator, he is damaged, and he damages the world with him. And if he rules over himself and unites himself with his Creator, and uses the world only to aid him in the service of his Creator, he is uplifted and the world itself is uplifted with him. For all creatures are greatly uplifted when they serve the "Whole Man," who is sanctified with the holiness of Hashem. It is as Chazal have said in relation to the light that Hashem stored away for the righteous (Chagiga 12a): "When Hashem saw the light that He had stored away for the righteous, He rejoiced, as it is said (Mishlei 13:9), `The light of the righteous rejoices.' " And in relation to the "stones of the place" that Jacob took and put around his head they said (Chulin 916), "R. Yitzchak said, `This teaches us that they [the stones] gathered themselves into one spot, each one saying, "Let the righteous one lay his head upon me." Chazal drew our attention to this principle in Midrash Koheleth, where they said (Koheleth Rabbah 7:28) - 'See the work of Hashem...' (Ecclesiastes 7:13). When Hashem created Adam, He took him and caused him to pass before all the trees of the Garden of Eden. He said to him, `See how beautiful and praiseworthy are my works; and all that I have created, I have created for your sake. Take heed that you do not damage and destroy my world.' "

To summarize, a man was created not for his station in this world, but for his station in the World to Come. It is only that his station in this world is a means toward his station in the World to Come, which is the ultimate goal. This accounts for numerous statements of Chazal, all in a similar vein, likening this world to the place and time of preparation, and the next world to the place which has been set aside for rest and for the eating of what has already been prepared. This is their intent in saying (Avos 4:21), "This world is similar to a corridor ...," as Chazal have said (Eruvin 22a), "Today for their performance and tomorrow to receive their reward," "He who exerted himself on Friday will eat on the Sabbath" (Avodah Zarah 3a), "This world is like the shore and the World to Come like the sea ..." (Koheleth Rabbah 1:36), and many other statements along the same lines.

And in truth, no reasoning being can believe that the purpose of man's creation relates to his station in this world. For what is a man's life in this world! Who is truly happy and content in this world? "The days of our life are seventy years, and, if exceedingly vigorous, eighty years, and their persistence is but labor and foolishness" (Tehillim 90:10). How many different kinds of suffering, and sicknesses, and pains and burdens! And after all this - death! Not one in a thousand is to be found to whom the world has yielded a superabundance of gratifications and true contentment. And even such a one, though he attain to the age of one hundred years, passes and vanishes from the world. Furthermore, if man had been created solely for the sake of this world, he would have had no need of being inspired with a soul so precious and exalted as to be greater than the angels themselves, especially so in that it derives no satisfaction whatsoever from all of the pleasures of this world. This is what Chazal teach us in Midrash (Koheleth Rabbah), "'And also the soul will not be filled' (Eccelesiastes 6:7) What is this analogous to? To the case of a city dweller who married a princess. If he brought her all that the world possessed, it would mean nothing to her, by virtue of her being a king's daughter. So is it with the soul. If it were to be brought all the delights of the world, they would be as nothing to it, in view of its pertaining to the higher elements." And so do Chazal say (Avos 4:29), "Against your will were you created, and against your will were you born." For the soul has no love at all for this world. To the contrary, it despises it. The Creator, Blessed be His Name, certainly would never have created something for an end which ran contrary to its nature and which it despised.

Man was created, then, for the sake of his station in the World to Come. Therefore, this soul was placed in him. For it befits the soul to serve Hashem; and through it a man may be rewarded in his place and in his time. And rather than the world's being despicable to the soul, it is, to the contrary, to be loved and desired by it. This is self-evident. After recognizing this we will immediately appreciate the greatness of the obligation that the mitzvos place upon us and the preciousness of the Divine service which lies in our hands. For these are the means which bring us to true perfection, a state which, without them, is unattainable. It is understood, however, that the attainment of a goal results only from a consolidation of all the available means employable toward its attainment, that the nature of a result is determined by the effectiveness and manner of employment of the means utilized toward its achievement, and that the slightest differentiation in the means will very noticeably affect the result to which they give rise upon the fruition of the aforementioned consolidation. This is self-evident.

It is obvious, then, that we must be extremely exacting in relation to the mitzvos and the service of Hashem, just as the weighers of gold and pearls are exacting because of the preciousness of these commodities. For their fruits result in true perfection and eternal wealth, than which nothing is more precious.

We thus derive that the essence of a man's existence in this world is solely the fulfilling of mitzvos, the serving of Hashem and the withstanding of trials, and that the world's pleasures should serve only the purpose of aiding and assisting him, by way of providing him with the contentment and peace of mind requisite for the freeing of his heart for the service which devolves upon him. It is indeed fitting that his every inclination be toward the Creator, may His Name be blessed, and that his every action, great or small, be motivated by no purpose other than that of drawing near to Hashem and breaking all the barriers (all the earthy elements and their concomitants) that stand between him and his Possessor, until he is pulled toward Hashem just as iron to a magnet. Anything that might possibly be a means to acquiring this closeness, he should pursue and clutch, and not let go of; and anything which might be considered a deterrent to it, he should flee as from a fire. As it is stated (Tehillim 63:9), "My soul clings to You; Your right hand sustains me." For a man enters the world only for this purpose - to achieve this closeness by rescuing his soul from all the deterrents to it and from all that detracts from it.

After we have recognized the truth of this principle, and it has become clear to us, we must investigate its details according to its stages, from beginning to end, as they were arranged by R. Pinchas ben Yair in the statement which has already been referred to in our introduction. These stages are: Watchfulness, Zeal, Cleanliness, Separation, Purity, Saintliness, Humility, Fear of Sin, and Holiness. And now, with the aid of Heaven, we will explain them one by one.

CHAPTER II

CONCERNING THE TRAIT OF WATCHFULNESS

THE IDEA OF WATCHFULNESS is for a man to exercise caution in his actions and his undertakings; that is, to deliberate and watch over his actions and his accustomed ways to determine whether or not they are good, so as not to abandon his soul to the danger of destruction, Hashem forbid, and not to walk according to the promptings of habit as a blind man in pitch darkness. This is demanded by one's intelligence. For considering the fact that a man possesses the knowledge and the reasoning ability to save himself and to flee from the destruction of his soul, is it conceivable that he would willingly blind himself to his own salvation? There is certainly no degradation and foolishness worse than this. One who does this is lower than beasts and wild animals, whose nature it is to protect themselves, to flee and to run away from anything that seems to endanger them. One who walks this world without considering whether his way of life is good or bad is like a blind man walking along the seashore, who is in very great danger, and whose chances of being lost are far greater than those of his being saved. For there is no difference between natural blindness and self-inflicted blindness, the shutting of one's eyes as an act of will and desire.

Jeremiah complains about the evil of the people of his generation, about their being affected with this affliction, the blinding of their eyes to their actions, their failure to analyze them in order to determine whether they should be engaged in or abandoned. He says about these people (Jeremiah 8:6), "No one regrets his wrongdoing, saying... They all turn away in their course as a horse rushing headlong into battle." He alludes here to their running on the impetus of their habits and their ways without leaving themselves time to evaluate their actions and ways,, and, as a result, falling into evil without noticing it. In reality, this is one of the clever devices of the evil inclination - to mount pressure unrelentingly against the hearts of people so as to leave them no leisure to consider and observe the type of life they are leading. For it realizes that if they were to devote even a slight degree of attention to their ways, there is no question but that they would immediately begin to repent of their deeds and that regret would wax in them until they would leave oft sinning altogether. It is this consideration which underlay the counsel of the wicked Pharaoh in his statement (Exodus 5:9), "Intensify the men's labors..." His intention was not merely to deprive them of all leisure so that they would not come to oppose him or plot against him, but he strove to strip their hearts of all thought by means of the enduring, interminable nature of their labor.

This is exactly the device that the evil inclination employs against man; for it is a warrior and well versed in deception. One cannot escape it without great wisdom and a broad outlook. As we are exhorted by the Prophet (Haggai 1:7), "Give heed to your ways." And as Solomon in his wisdom said (Mishlei 6:4), "Give neither sleep to your eyes nor slumber to your eyelids. Rescue yourself as a deer from the hand..." And as Chazal said (Sotah 5b), "All who deliberate upon their paths in this world will be worthy to witness the salvation wrought by Hashem." Clearly even if one superintends himself, it is not within his power to save himself without the help of Hashem. For the evil inclination is extremely tenacious, as Scripture states (Tehillim 37:32), "The wicked one looks to the righteous and seeks to kill him; Hashem will not leave him... " If a man looks to himself, Hashem helps him, and he is saved from the evil inclination. But if he gives no heed to himself, Hashem will certainly not superintend him; for if he does not pity himself, who should pity him? This is as Chazal have said (Berachoth 33a), "It is forbidden to pity anyone who has no understanding," and (Avos 1:14), "If I am not for myself, who will be for me?"

CHAPTER III

CONCERNING THE DIVISIONS OF WATCHFULNESS

ONE WHO WISHES to watch over himself must take two things into consideration. First he must consider what constitutes the true good that a person should choose and the true evil that he should flee from; and second, he must consider his actions, to discover whether they appertain to the category of good or to that of evil. This applies both to times when there is a question of performing a specific action and to times when there is no such question. When there is a question of performing a specific action, he should do nothing before he weighs the action in the scale of the aforementioned understanding. And when there is no such question, the idea should take the form of his bringing before himself the remembrance of his deeds in general and weighing them, likewise, in the scales of this criterion to determine what they contain of evil, so that he may cast it aside, and what of good, so that he may be constant in it and strengthen himself in it. If he finds in them aught that is evil, he should consider and attempt to reason out what device he might use to turn aside from that evil and to cleanse himself of it. Chazal taught us this in their statement (Eruvin 136), "It would have been better for a man not to have been created... but now that he has been created, let him examine his deeds. Others say, `Let him "feel" his deeds.' " It is to be seen that these two versions constitute two sound beneficial exhortations. For "examination" of one's deeds refers to an investigation of one's deeds in general and a consideration of them to determine whether they might not include certain actions which should not be performed, which are not in accordance with Hashem's mitzvos and His statutes, any such actions to be completely eradicated. "Feeling," however, implies the investigation even of the good actions themselves to determine whether they involve any leaning which is not good or any bad aspect which it is necessary to remove and to eradicate. This is analogous to a person's feeling a garment to determine whether its material is good and sturdy or weak and rotted. In the same respect he must "feel" his actions by subjecting them to a most exhaustive examination to determine their nature, so that he might remain free of any impurities.

To summarize, a man should observe all of his actions and watch over all of his ways so as not to leave himself with a bad habit or a bad trait, let alone a sin or a crime. I see a need for a person to carefully examine his ways and to weigh them daily in the manner of the great merchants who constantly evaluate all of their undertakings so that they do not miscarry. He should set aside definite times and hours for this weighing so that it is not a fortuitous matter, but one which is conducted with the greatest regularity; for it yields rich returns.

Chazal have explicitly taught us the need for such an evaluation. As they said (Bava Bathra 78b), "Therefore the rulers say, `Let us enter into an accounting' (Numbers 21:27). Therefore the rulers over their evil inclinations say, 'Let us come and compute the world's account, the loss entailed by the performance of a mitzvah, against the gain that one secures through it, and the gain that one acquires through a transgression against the loss that it entails... '

This true counsel could not have been given, nor its truth recognized by any except those who had already departed from beneath the hand of their evil inclination and come to dominate it. For if one is still imprisoned by his evil inclination, his eyes cannot see this truth and he cannot recognize it. For the evil inclination literally blinds his eyes and he becomes as one who walks in the darkness, where there are stumbling blocks before him which his eyes do not see. As Chazal said (Bava Metzia 83b), " ` You laid down darkness and it was night' (Tehillim 104:20). This refers to this world which is similar to night." How wondrous is this truthful commentary to him who concentrates upon understanding it. For the darkness of night can cause two types of errors in relation to a man's eye: it may either cover his eye so that he does not see what is before him at all, or it may deceive him so that a pillar appears to him as a man, or a man as a pillar. In like manner, the earthiness and materialism of this world is the darkness of night to the mind's eye and causes a man to err in two ways. First it does not permit him to see the stumbling blocks in the ways of the world, so that the fools walk securely, fall, and are lost without having experienced any prior fear. As Scripture states (Mishlei 4:19), "The path of the wicked is like pitch darkness; they do not know upon what they stumble," and (Mishlei 22:3), "The wise man sees the evil and hides, and the fools pass on and are punished," and (Mishlei 14:16), "The fool becomes infuriated and is secure." For their hearts are steadfast and they fall before having any knowledge of the existence of the stumbling block. The second error, which is even worse than the first, stems from the distortion of their sight - they see evil as though it were goodness itself, and good as if it were evil, and, because of this, strengthen themselves in clinging to their evil ways. For it is not enough that they lack the ability to see the truth, the evil staring them in the face, but they also see fit to find powerful substantiations and empirical evidence supporting their evil theories and false ideas. This is the great evil which embraces them and brings them to destruction. As Scripture states (Isaiah 6:10), "The heart of this nation has become fatted, and its ears have become heavy, and its eyes have turned aside, lest..." All this because of their being under the influence of the darkness and subject to the rule of their evil inclination. But those who have already freed themselves from this bondage see the truth clearly and can advise others in relation to it.

To what is this analogous? To a garden-maze, a type of garden common among the ruling class, which is planted for the sake of amusement. The plants there are arranged in walls between which are found many confusing and interlacing paths, all similar to one another, the purpose of the whole being to challenge one to reach a portico in their midst. Some of the paths are straight ones which lead directly to the portico, but some cause one to stray, and to wander from it. The walker between the paths has no way of seeing or knowing whether he is on the true or the false path; for they are all similar, presenting no difference whatsoever to the observing eye. He will not reach his goal unless he has perfect familiarity and visual acquaintance with the paths through his having traversed them and reached the portico. He who occupies a commanding position in the portico, however, sees all of the paths before him and can discriminate between the true and the false ones. He is in a position to warn those who walk upon them and to tell them, "This is the path; take it!" He who is willing to believe him will reach the designated spot; but he who is not willing to believe him, but would rather trust to his eyes, will certainly remain lost and fail to reach it.

So too in relation to the idea under discussion. He who has not yet achieved dominion over his evil inclination is in the midst of the paths and cannot distinguish between them. But those who rule their evil inclination, those who have reached the portico, who have already left the paths and who clearly see all of the ways before their eyes - they can advise him who is willing to listen, and it is to them that we must trust.

And what is the advice that they give us'? - 'Let us enter into an accounting.' Let us come and compute the world's account." For they have already experienced, and seen, and learned that this alone is the true path by which a man may reach the good that he seeks, and that there is none beside this.

What emerges from all this is that a man must constantly - at all times, and particularly during a regularly appointed time of solitude - reflect upon the true path (according to the ordinance of the Torah) that a man must walk upon. After engaging in such reflection he will come to consider whether or not his deeds travel along this path. For in doing so it will certainly be easy for him to cleanse himself of all evil and to correct all of his ways. As Scripture states (Mishlei 4:26), "Consider the path of your feet and all of your paths will be established," and (Lamentations 3:40), "Let us seek out our ways and examine them, and we will return to Hashem."

CHAPTER IV

CONCERNING THE MANNER OF ACQUIRING WATCHFULNESS

THAT WHICH, in general, brings a person to Watchfulness is Torah study. As R. Pinchas stated in the beginning of the Baraitha, "Torah brings one to Watchfulness." That which leads to it specifically, however, is reflection upon the demanding nature of the Divine service that a man is responsible for and the severity of the judgment which it involves. This understanding may be gained by analyzing the incidents that are related in the sacred writings and by studying the statements of the Sages of blessed memory which awaken one to it.

In this process of understanding, there are various levels of ideas, applying respectively to those with wholeness of understanding, those of lesser understanding and the general populace.

Those with wholeness of understanding will be primarily motivated toward Watchfulness by their coming to see clearly that only perfection and nothing else is worthy of their desire and that there is no worse evil than the lack of and removal from perfection. For after this has become clear to them, as well as the fact that the means to this end are virtuous deeds and traits, they will certainly never permit themselves to diminish these means; nor will they ever fail to make use of their [the means'] full potential. For it would already have become clear to them that if these means were reduced in number or not employed with complete effectiveness, with all of the energy that they called for, true perfection would not be attained through them, but would be lacked to the extent that sufficient exertion was lacking in relation to them. There is no misfortune nor any evil that those with wholeness of understanding deem greater than this lack of perfection. They will, therefore, choose to increase the number of these means and to be rigid in relation to all of their aspects. They will find no rest or peace from the worry that they possibly lack something which might lead them to the perfection that they desire. As was said by King Solomon, may Peace be upon him (Mishlei 28:14), "Happy is the man who always fears." Our Sages (Berachoth 60a) interpreted this statement as applying to the realm of Torah. The trait to which this degree of attainment leads is the one which is termed "Fear of Sin," a trait which constitutes one of the highest levels of achievement. Its intent is that a man constantly fear and worry lest he be harboring a trace of sin which might keep him from the perfection that he is dutybound to strive for. Concerning this Chazal said by way of analogy (Bava Bathra 75a), "This teaches us that everyone is burned by his neighbor's canopy." It is not jealousy which is the operative factor here (for jealousy as I will explain further with the help of Heaven, is encountered only among those who lack understanding), but rather the fact that he sees himself as lacking a level of achievement toward perfection, a level that he could have attained just as his neighbor had. If he who possesses wholeness of understanding engages in this thought process, he certainly will not fall short of being watchful in his deeds.

Those of lesser understanding, however, will be motivated toward Watchfulness according to their particular level of discrimination, so that their quest will be for the honor that they desire. It is evident to every man of faith that the different stations in the World of Truth, the World to Come, vary only in relation to one's deeds; that only he who is greater in deeds than his neighbor will be elevated above him, whereas he who is lesser in deeds will occupy a lower level. How, then, can a man blind his eyes to his actions or slacken his efforts, if afterwards, when he can no longer straighten out what he has made crooked, he will unquestionably suffer?

There are some fools who seek only to lighten their burden. They say, "Why weary ourselves with so much Saintliness and Separation? Is it not enough for us that we will not be numbered among the wicked who are judged in Gehinnom? We will not force ourselves to enter all the way into Paradise. If we do not have a large portion, we will have a small one. It will be enough for us. We will not add to our burdens for the sake of greater acquisitions." There is one question that we will ask these people -could they so easily, in this transitory world, tolerate the sight of one of their friends being honored, and elevated above them, and coming to rule over them-or, more so, one of their servants or one of the paupers who are shameful and lowly in their eyes? Could they tolerate this without suffering and without their blood boiling in them? Is there any question that they could not? We witness with our own eyes all of the labors of a man to elevate himself above everyone he can and to establish his place among the exalted. This is a man's jealousy of his neighbor. If he sees his neighbor elevated while he remains low, what he tolerates will be what he is forced to tolerate because of his inability to alter the situation: but his heart will brood within him. If it is so difficult, then, for them to abide being on a lower level than others in respect to qualities whose desirability is illusive and deceitful, qualities in relation to which a man's being designated as lowly is but a surface judgment, and his being elevated, vanity and falsity, then how could they tolerate seeing themselves lower than those same persons who are now lower than they? And this in the place of true quality and everlasting worth, which, though they might not give heart to it now because of their failure to recognize it and its value, they will certainly recognize in its time for what it is, to their grief and shame. There is no question that their suffering will be terrible and interminable. This tolerance, then, that they adopt in order to lighten their burden is nothing but a deceitful persuasion of their evil inclination, with no basis whatsoever in truth. If they saw the truth, there would be no room for such deception, but because they do not seek it, but walk and stray according to their desires, these persuasions will not leave them until such a time when it will no longer avail them, when it will no longer be in their hands to rebuild what they have destroyed. As was said by King Solomon, may Peace be upon him (Ecclesiastes 9:10), "Whatever your hand finds to do with your strength, do it, for there is no deed, nor account, nor knowledge..." That is, what a man does not do while he still has the power that His Creator has given him (the power of choice that is given to him to employ during his lifetime, when he can exercise free will and is commanded to do so) he will not again have the opportunity of doing in the grave and in the pit, for at that time he will no longer possess this power. For one who has not multiplied good deeds in his lifetime will not have the opportunity of performing them afterwards. And one who has not taken an accounting of his deeds will not have time to do so later. And one who has not become wise in this world will not become wise in the grave. This is the intent of (Ibid.) ". .. for there is no deed nor account nor knowledge nor wisdom in the pit to which you are going."

But the general populace will be motivated toward Watchfulness through a recognition of the depth of judgment in relation to reward and punishment. In truth, one should continuously tremble and shiver, for who will abide the Day of Judgment, and who will be deemed righteous before his Creator, whose scrutiny dissects all things, small and great. As Chazal have said (Chagigah 5b), " `And He relates to a man his conversation' (Amos 4:13). Even a casual conversation between a man and his wife is related to him at the time of judgment." And, similarly, (Yevamoth 121b), " `And around Him it storms violently' (Tehillim 50: 3). This teaches us that Hashem judges His Tzaddikim to the degree of a hair's-breadth" [an inference derived from the structural relationship between "storms" and "hair" in the Hebrew].

Abraham - the same Abraham who was so beloved by his Possessor that Scripture (Isaiah 41:8) refers to him as "Abraham, my beloved" - Abraham did not escape judgment for a slight indiscretion in his use of words. Because he said, (Bereishis 15:8), "With what shall I know," Hashem said to him, "Upon your life, you shall surely know, for your children will be strangers..." (Vayikra Rabbah 11:5). And because he entered into a covenant with Avimelech without having been commanded by G -d to do so, Hashem, said to him, "Upon your life, I shall delay the rejoicing of your sons for seven generations" (Bereshith Rabbah 54:5).

Jacob, because he became angry with Rachel upon her saying to him (Bereishis 30:1), "Give me sons," was told by Hashem, "Is this the way to answer those who are oppressed? Upon your life, your sons will stand before her son" (Bereshith Rabbah 71: 10). And because he placed Dinah in a chest so that Esau would not seize her, even though his intentions in doing so were unquestionably worthy ones, we are told in the Midrash (Ibid. 80:3) that Hashem said to him, because he withheld kindliness from his brother, " `Who keeps kindliness from his neighbor' (Job 6:14) - Because you did not wish to wed her lawfully, she will be wed unlawfully."

Joseph, because he said to the one appointed over the drink (Bereishis 40:14), "But remember me in relation to yourself," had two years added to his imprisonment, as we are told by Chazal (Bereshith Rabbah 89:2). Also, because he embalmed his father without Hashem's permission, or, according to a second opinion, because he heard, "Your servant, our father" and kept still, he died before his brothers (Bereshith Rabbah 100:3).

David, because he referred to words of Torah as "songs," was punished by having his joy dampened through Uzzah's indiscretion (Sotah 35a).

Michal, because she admonished David for dancing in public before the ark, was punished by dying in childbirth, having had no other children in her lifetime (II Samuel 6:20 f).

Hezekiah - because he revealed the treasure house to the officers of the Babylonian king, it was decreed that his sons serve as eunuchs in the palace of the King of Babylonia. (II Kings 20:12 ff).

There are many more instances of this nature.

In the chapter "All are Liable" (Chagiga 5a), Chazal told us, "Rabbi Yochanan cried when he came to the following verse (Malachi 3:5): `And I will draw near to you in judgment, and I will be a quick witness...' Is there any remedy for a servant against whom lesser offenses are weighed, as grave ones are?" It is certainly not the point of this statement that the punishment is identical for both, for Hashem pays measure for measure. It is rather to be understood that in relation to the weighing of deeds, those which are less weighty are placed upon the balance just as the weightier ones are; for the latter will not cause the former to be forgotten, nor will the Judge overlook them, just as He will not overlook the weighty ones. But He will consider and attend to all of these equally, judging each one of them and meting out punishment for each one according to its nature. As was said by King Solomon, may Peace be upon him (Ecclesiastes 12:14), "For G -d will bring every deed into judgment." Just as Hashem does not allow any good deed, small as it may be, to go unrewarded, so does He not permit any bad deed, however small, to go unjudged and unpassed upon, contrary to the thinking of those who wish to talk it into themselves that Hashem Blessed be He, will not review the lighter things in His judgment and will not call them into account. It is an acknowledged principle (Bava Kamma 50a): "Whoever says that Hashem overlooks things will have his life `overlooked.' " And Chazal have also said (Chagiga Iba), "If the evil inclination says to you, `Sin and Hashem will forgive you,' do not heed it." All this is obvious and clear, for G -d is a G- d of truth. It is this idea which is embodied in the statement of Moshe our Teacher, may Peace be upon him (Dvarim 32:4), "The Rock-His work is whole; for all of His ways are just. He is a Hashem of faithfulness, without wrong. . ." Since Hashem desires justice, ignoring the bad would be as much of an injustice as ignoring the good. If He desires justice, then, He must deal with each man according to his ways and according to the fruits of his acts, with the most minute discrimination, for good or for bad. This is what underlies the statement of Chazal (Yalkut Ibid.) that the verse "He is a Hashem of faithfulness, without wrong; He is righteous and just" has application to the righteous and to the wicked. For this is His attribute. He judges everything. He punishes every sin. There is no escaping.

To those who might ask at this point, "Seeing that whatever the case may be, everything must be subjected to judgment, what function does the attribute of mercy perform?" the answer is that the attribute of mercy is certainly the mainstay of the world; for the world could not exist at all without it. Nevertheless the attribute of justice is not affected. For on the basis of justice alone it would be dictated that the sinner be punished immediately upon sinning, without the least delay; that the punishment itself be a wrathful one, as befits one who rebels against the word of the Creator, blessed be His Name; and that there be no correction whatsoever for the sin. For in truth, how can a man straighten what has been made crooked after the commission of the sin? If a man killed his neighbor; if he committed adultery-how can he correct this? Can he remove the accomplished fact from actuality?

It is the attribute of mercy which causes the reverse of the three things we have mentioned. That is, it provides that the sinner be given time, and not be wiped out as soon as he sins; that the punishment itself not involve utter destruction; and that the gift of repentance be given to sinners with absolute lovingkindness, so that the rooting out of the will which prompted the deed be considered a rooting out of the deed itself. That is, when he who is repenting recognizes his sin, and admits it, and reflects upon his evil, and repents, and wishes that the sin had never been committed, as he would wish that a certain vow had never been made, in which case there is complete regret, and he desires and yearns that the deed had never been done, and suffers great anguish in his heart because of its already having been done, and departs from it for the future, and flees from itthen the uprooting of the act from his will is accredited to him as the uprooting of a vow, and he gains atonement. As Scripture states (Isaiah 6:7), "Your wrong will depart, and your sin will be forgiven." The wrong actually departs from existence and is uprooted because of his suffering for and regretting now what had taken place in the past. This is certainly a function of lovingkindness and not of justice. In any event, however, it is a type of lovingkindness which does not entirely negate the attribute of justice. It can be seen as according with justice in that in place of the act of will from which the sin arose and the pleasure that it afforded, there is now regret and suffering. So, too, the time extension constitutes not a pardoning of the sin, but rather Hashem's bearing with the sinner for a while to open the door of repentance to him. Similarly, all of the other operations of lovingkindness, such as "The son benefits his father," (Sunhedrin 104x) and "Part of a life is like the whole life" (Kcheleth Rabbah 7:48), mentioned by our Sages, are aspects of lovingkindness wherein small amounts are accounted large. But these considerations do not militate against nor actually negate the attribute of justice, for there is good reason to attach importance to them.

But for sins to be pardoned or ignored would be entirely contrary to the concept of justice, for then there would be no judgment and no true law in relation to things. It is, therefore, impossible for such a situation to obtain. And if the sinner does not find open to him one of the avenues of escape that we have mentioned, it is certain that the attribute of justice will not emerge empty-handed. As Chazal have said (Yerushalmi Ta'anith 2:1), "He withholds His wrath, but He collects what is His."

We see, then, that the man who wants to open his eyes to the truth can offer himself no possible argument for not exercising the maximum of Watchfulness in his deeds and subjecting them to the most thorough analysis.

All of these are observations which, if one approaches them with sensitivity, will certainly lead him to the acquisition of Watchfulness.

CHAPTER V

CONCERNING THE FACTORS WHICH DETRACT FROM WATCHFULNESS AND THE WITHDRAWING OF ONESELF FROM THEM

THE FACTORS which detract from this trait and withdraw one from it are three: The first is worldly occupation and involvement, the second, laughter and levity, and the third, evil companionship. We will discuss each one individually.

We have already discussed worldly occupation and involvement. When a man is involved in worldly affairs, his thoughts are bound by the chains of the burden that weighs upon them and it is impossible for them to become concerned with his deeds. The Sages, may Peace be upon them, said, in their awareness of this fact (Avos 4.10), "Minimize your occupations and occupy yourself with Torah." A person must occupy himself to a certain extent for the sake of a livelihood, but not to the extent where his Divine service is interfered with. It is in respect to this that we were commanded to set aside times for Torah study. We have already mentioned that it is such study which is the prime requirement for Watchfulness; as stated by R. Pinhas, "Torah brings one to Watchfulness." Without it, Watchfulness will not be attained. As Chazal have stated (Avos 2.6), "An ignoramus cannot be a saint." This is true because the very Creator, Blessed be His name, who invested man with an evil inclination, created the Torah as an antidote to it (Kiddushin 30b). It is self-evident that if the Creator has fashioned for this affliction only this remedy, it is impossible under any circumstances that a person be cured of it through any other means. One who thinks to save himself without it is mistaken, and will recognize his mistake only in the end, when he dies in sin. For the evil inclination exerts great force against a person, and, without his being aware of it, grows and waxes stronger, and comes to dominate him. A man may resort to all the devices imaginable - if he does not adopt the remedy which was created for him, namely, the Torah, as I have written, he will neither recognize nor feel the intensification of his illness until he dies in sin and his soul is lost.

To what is this analogous? To the case of a sick man, who, consulting doctors and having his sickness correctly diagnosed and prescribed for, nevertheless, possessing no previous knowledge of medicine, abandons their prescription and takes instead whatever medicine he happens to think of. Is there any doubt that he will die?

The same is true in our case. No one understands the disease of the evil inclination and the potentialities inherent within it but the Creator who fashioned it. And He Himself cautioned us that the only antidote to it is Torah. Who, then, can abandon it and take anything else and expect to live? The darkness of earthiness will advance upon him degree by degree without his sensing it, until he finds himself sunk in evil and so far removed from truth that it will not even occur to him to seek it. If, however, he occupies himself with Torah, then, when he sees its ways, its commandments and its warnings, there will awaken within him responses which will lead him to the ways of good. As Chazal have said (Yerushalmi Chagigah 1:7), "Would that they left me and kept my Torah, for the radiance within it would return them to good."

Also included in this category is the setting aside of times for consideration of one's deeds, with an eye toward their correction, as I wrote above. In addition to this, he who is wise will not permit any time that may remain from his affairs to go lost, but he will immediately seize it, and not let it go, in order to employ it toward self-improvement and the betterment of his Divine service.

The deterrent that we have been discussing, though more common than the others, is the easiest to escape, for those who wish to escape it. The second deterrent, however, laughter and levity, is very severe. He who is immersed in it is as one who is immersed in a great ocean, from which it is extremely difficult to escape. For laughter affects a person's heart in such a manner that sense and reason no longer prevail in him, so that he becomes like a drunkard or a simpleton, whom, because they cannot accept direction, it is impossible to advise or direct. As was said by King Solomon, may Peace be upon him (Ecclesiastes 2:2), "About laughter I have said, `It is silly,' and about happiness, `What does it do?"' And Chazal have said (Avos 3.13), "Laughter and lightheadedness motivate a man toward illicit relations." For even though every reasoning individual recognizes the gravity of this kind of sin and his heart is afraid to approach it because of the vividness of the impression that has stamped itself into his mind, of the truly terrible nature of the offense and the severity of its punishment, still laughter and lightheadedness draw him on little by little and lead him closer and closer to the stage where fear leaves him little by little, degree by degree, until finally he reaches the sin itself and commits it. Why is this so? Just as the essence of Watchfulness involves applying one's heart to things, so the essence of laughter is the turning away of one's heart from just, attentive thinking, so that thoughts of fearing Hashem do not enter one's heart at all.

Consider the great severity and destructive power of levity. Like a shield smeared with oil, which wards off arrows and causes them to fall to the ground, not permitting them to reach the bearer's body, is levity in the face of reproof and rebuke. For with one bit of levity and with a little laughter a person can cast from himself the great majority of the awakenings and impressions that a man's heart stimulates and effects within itself upon his seeing or hearing things which arouse him to an acconting and an examination of his deeds. The force of levity flings everything to the ground so that no impression whatsoever is made upon Him. This is due not to the weakness of the forces playing upon him, nor to any lack of understanding on his part, but to the power of levity, which obliterates all facets of moral evaluation and fear of Hashem. Touching this the Prophet Isaiah "screamed like a crane," for he saw that it was this which left no place for his exhortations to make an impression and which destroyed all hope for the sinners. As it is stated (Isaiah 28:22), "And now do not engage in levity lest your bonds be strengthened." And our Sages have pronounced (Avodah Zarah 18b) that one who is given to levity brings suffering upon himself. Scripture itself explicity states (Mishlei 19:29), "Judgments are appropriate for the light-headed." Indeed, this is dictated by reason; for one who is influenced by thought and studies does not require bodily punishment, for he will leave off sinning without it by virtue of the thoughts of repentance which will arise in his heart through what he will read or hear of moral judgments and exhortations. But the light-headed, who because of the force of their levity are not influenced by exhortations cannot be corrected except through punitive judgments. For their levity will not be as effective in warding off these as it is in warding off ethical appeals. In accordance with the severity of the sin and its consequences is the True Judge severe in His punishment. As Chazal have taught us (Avodah Zarah 18b), "The punishment for levity is extremely severe; it begins with suffering and ends with destruction, as it is said (Isaiah 28:22), `Lest your bonds be strengthened, for I have heard destruction and cutting off..."

The third deterrent to Watchfulness is evil companionship, that is, the companionship of fools and sinners, as Scripture states (Mishlei 13:20), "And the friend of fools will be broken." Very often we see that even after the truth of a man's responsibility for Divine service and Watchfulness has impressed itself upon a person, he weakens or commits certain trespasses in order not to be mocked by his friends or to be able to mix freely with them. This is the intent of Solomon's warning (Mishlei 24:21), "Do not mix with those who make changes." If someone says to you (Kethuvoth 17a), "A man's mind should always be associated with his fellow men," tell him, "This refers to people who conduct themselves as human beings and not to people who conduct themselves as animals." Solomon again warns (Mishlei 14:7), "Withdraw yourself from a fool." And King David said in this connection (Tehillim 1: 1), "Happy is the man who did not walk...... upon which Chazal have commented (Avodah Zarah 18b), "If he walked he will eventually stand, and if he stood, he will eventually sit." And again (Tehillim 26:4), "I have not sat with false people ...I despised the society of the wicked ..." What a person must do, then, is to purify and cleanse himself, and keep his feet from the paths of the crowd who are immersed in the foolishness of the time, and turn them to the precincts of Hashem and His dwelling places. As David himself concludes (Ibid. 6), "I will wash my hands in cleanliness, and I will go round Your altar, O G -d." If there are among his companions those who subject him to ridicule, he should not take it to heart, but, to the contrary, should ridicule them and shame them. Let him consider whether, if he had the opportunity of acquiring a great deal of money, he would keep from undertaking what such acquisition entailed so as to avoid the ridicule of his companions. How much more averse should he be to losing his soul for the sake of sparing himself ridicule. In this connection Chazal exhorted us (Aroth 5.23), "Be fierce as a leopard to do the will of your Father in heaven." And David said (Tehillim 119:46), "And I will speak of your testimonies before kings and I will not be ashamed." Even though most of the kings of his time occupied themselves with, and were wont to converse upon grandiose schemes and pleasures, and we would, therefore, tend to expect that David, himself a king, would be ashamed, while in their presence, to speak of ethical questions and Torah instead of discussing great feats and the pleasures of people such as they - in spite of all this, David was not in the least perturbed, and his heart was not seduced by these vanities, because he had already attained to the truth. He states explicitly (Tehillim 119:46), "And I will speak of your testimonies before kings and I will not be ashamed." Isaiah, likewise, said (Isaiah 50:7), "I therefore made my face like flint and I knew that I would not be ashamed."

CHAPTER VI

CONCERNING THE TRAIT OF ZEAL

AFTER WATCHFULNESS comes Zeal, Watchfulness pertaining to the negative commandments and Zeal to the positive, in accordance with the idea of "Depart from evil and do good (Tehillim 34:15)." "Zeal," as the name implies, signifies alacrity in the pursuit and fulfillment of mitzvos. As expressed by Chazal (Pesachim 4a), "The zealous advance themselves toward mitzvos." That is, just as it requires great intelligence and much foresight to save oneself from the snares of the evil inclination and to escape from evil so that it does not come to rule us and intrude itself into our deeds, so does it require great intelligence and foresight to take hold of mitzvos, to acquire them for ourselves, and not to lose them. For just as the evil inclination attempts, with the devices at its command, to cast a man into the nets of sin, so does it seek to prevent him from performing mitzvos, and to leave Him devoid of them. If a man weakens and is lazy and does not strengthen himself to pursue mitzvos and to hold onto them, he will certainly lack them.

A person's nature exercises a strong downward pull upon him. This is so because the grossness which characterizes the substance of earthiness keeps a man from desiring exertion and labor. One who wishes, therefore, to attain to the service of the Creator, may His Name be blessed, must strengthen himself against his nature and be zealous. If he leaves himself in the hands of his downward- pulling nature, there is no question that he will not succeed. As the Tanna says "Be fierce as a leopard, light as an eagle, swift as a deer and strong as a lion to do the will of your Father in heaven." Chazal have numbered Torah and good deeds among those things which require self-fortification (Berachoth 32b). And Scripture plainly states (Joshua 1:7), "Strengthen yourself and be very courageous to observe to do according to all the Torah which Moshe My servant commanded you." One who seeks to transform his nature completely requires great strengthening. Solomon repeatedly exhorts us concerning this, recognizing the evil of laziness and the greatness of the loss that results from it. He says (Mishlei 6:10), "A little sleep, a little slumber, a little folding of the hands to sleep and your poverty is suddenly upon you and your want as an armed man." The lazy man, though not actively evil, produces evil through his very inactivity. We read further (Mishlei 18:9), "Also he who slackens in his work is a brother to the Destroyer." Though he is not the Destroyer who commits the evil with his own hands, let him not think that he is far-removed from him - he is his blood-brother.

A portrayal of a daily occurrence furnishes us with a clear idea of the lazy man's wickedness (Mishlei 24:30.). "I passed by the field of a lazy man and by the vineyard of a man without sense and it was overgrown with thistles; its face was covered with nettles... And I beheld; I put my heart to it; I saw; I took instruction, a little sleep, a little slumber ... and suddenly your poverty is upon you ..." Aside from the surface description, whereby we are provided with an unquestionably true account of what happens to the lazy man's field, a very beautiful interpretation has been put forth by Chazal (Yalkut Shimoni Mishlei 961): " `and it was overgrown with thistles' - he seeks the interpretation of a passage and does not find it; ,its face was covered' - because of his not having labored in the Law, he sits in judgment and declares the pure, unclean and the impure, clean, and he breaches the fences of the Scholars. What is this man's punishment? Solomon tells us (Ecclesiastes 10:8) : `One who breaches a fence will be bitten by a snake.' " That is, the evil of the lazy man does not come all at once, but little by little, without his recognizing and sensing it. He is pulled from evil to evil until he finds himself sunk in evil's very depths. He begins by not expending the amount of effort which could be expected of him. This causes him not to study Torah as he should; and because of this, when he later does come to study it, he lacks the requisite understanding. It would be bad enough if his evil were to end here, but it does not. It grows even worse; for in his desire, notwithstanding, to interpret the section or chapter under consideration, he adduces interpretations which are not in accordance with the law, destroys the truth and perverts it, trespasses upon ordinances, and breaches the fences. His end, like that of all who breach fences, is destruction. Solomon continues (Ibid.), "And I beheld; I put my heart to it" - I thought upon this thing and I saw the terrible nature of the evil in it; it is like a poison which continues to spread, little by little, its workings unnoticed, until death results. This is the meaning of "A little sleep ... and suddenly your poverty is upon you as an armed man ..."

We see with our own eyes how often a person neglects his duty in spite of his awareness of it and in spite of his having come to recognize as a truth what is required for the salvation of his soul and what is incumbent upon him in respect to his Creator. This neglect is due not to an inadequate recognition of his duty nor to any other cause but the increasing weight of his laziness upon him; so that he says, "I will eat a little," or "I will sleep a little," or "It is hard for me to leave the house," or "I have taken off my shirt, how can I put it on again?" (Canticles 5:3). "It is very hot outside," "It is very cold," or "It is raining too hard" and all the other excuses and pretenses that the mouth of fools is full of. Either way, the Torah is neglected, Divine service dispensed with, and the Creator abandoned. As Solomon said (Ecclesiastes 10:18), "Through laziness the roof sinks in, and through the hands' remaining low, the house leaks." If his laziness is held up to him, the lazy man will doubtless come back with many quotations culled from the Sages and from Scripture, and with intellectual arguments, all supporting, according to his misguided mind, his leniency with himself (and all allowing him to remain in the repose of his laziness). He fails to see that these arguments and explanations stem not from rational evaluation, but from his laziness, which, when it grows strong within him, inclines his reason and intelligence to them, so that he does not pay heed to what is said by the wise and by those who possess sound judgment. It is in this connection that Solomon cried (Mishlei 26:16), "A lazy man is wiser in his own eyes than seven sages!" Laziness does not even permit one to attend to the words of those who reprove him; he puts them all down for blunderers and fools, reckoning only himself wise.

A principle that experience has shown to be of central importance to the work of Separation is that whatever tends to lighten one's burden must be examined carefully. For although such alleviation is sometimes justified and reasonable, it is most often a deceitful prescription of the evil inclination, and must, therefore, be subjected to much analysis and investigation. If, after such an examination, it still seems justified, then it is certainly acceptable.

In fine, a man must greatly strengthen himself, and power himself with Zeal to perform the mitzvos, casting from himself the hindering weight of laziness. The angels were extolled for their Zeal, as is said of them (Tehillim 103:20), "Mighty in power, they do His word, to listen to the voice of His word," and (Ezekiel 1:14), "And the living creatures ran and returned, as streaks of lightning." A man is a man and not an angel, and it is therefore impossible for him to attain to the strength of an angel, but he should surely strive to come as close to that level as his nature allows. King David, grateful for his portion of Zeal, said (Tehillim 119:60), "I was quick; I did not delay in keeping Your mitzvos."

CHAPTER VII

CONCERNING THE DIVISIONS OF ZEAL

THERE ARE TWO DIVISIONS OF ZEAL, one relating to the period before, and the other to the period after the beginning of the deed. The concern of the former is that a man not permit a mitzvah to grow stale, that when the time for its performance arrives, or when it happens to present itself to him, or when the thought of performing it enters his mind, he make haste to take hold of the mitzvah and perform it, and not allow much time to elapse in the interim, there being no greater danger; for each new minute can bring with it some new hindrance to a good deed. Chazal awakened us to this truth through reference to the coronation of Solomon (Bereshith Rabbah 76:2), in relation to which David told Benaiah (I Kings 1:33,36), "...and take him down to Gichon," and Benaiah answered, "Amen, may Hashem say so ." "R. Pinchas asked in the name of R. Chanan of Sepphoris, `Was it not said (I Chronicles 22:9), "A son will be born to you and he will be a man of peace?" The answer is: Many adverse occurrences can take place from here to Gichon.' " We were therefore warned by Chazal (Mechilta Shemoth 12:17), " `Watch over the matzoth' - if a mitzvah presents itself to you, do not permit it to go stale;" and (Nazir 23b), "A man should always advance himself toward a mitzvah, for because the elder daughter preceded the younger she was worthy of putting forward four generations of royalty in Israel;" and (Pesachim 4a), "The zealous advance themselves toward mitzvos;" and (Berachoth 66), "A man should always run to perform a mitzvah, even on Shabbos." And in the Midrash it is stated, (Vayikra Rabbah 11:8), " `He will guide us eternally '(Tehillim 48:15), - with Zeal, as young maids ["eternally" and "young maids" are similarly constructed in the Hebrew], as it is said (Tehillim 68:26), '... in the midst of young maids playing upon timbrels."' The possession of Zeal constitutes an extremely high level of spiritual development, which a person's nature prevents him from attaining at once. He who strengthens himself, however, and acquires as much of Zeal as he is able to, will, in time to come, truly attain to it. The Creator, may His Name be blessed, will present it to him as a reward for having striven for it during the time of his service.

The concern of "Zeal after the beginning of the deed" is that a man, after taking hold of a mitzvah, make haste to complete it; not for the sake of ease, as with one who wishes to relieve himself of a burden, but for fear that he might not otherwise be able to complete it. Chazal have voiced many exhortations concerning this: (Bereshith Rabbah 85:4), "One who begins a mitzvah and does not complete it buries his wife and sons;" and (Ibid.), "A mitzvah is attributed only to the one who completes it." And King Solomon, may Peace be upon him, said (Mishlei 22:29), "Have you seen a man quick in his work? He will stand before kings. He will not stand before low -life." Chazal paid this tribute to Solomon himself (Sanhedrin 104b) for having made haste in the building of the Temple, and not having idled and delayed it. They commented in a similar manner upon Moshe' zeal in the work of the Tabernacle (Shir Hashirim Rabbah 1:2).

It is to be observed that all of the deeds of the righteous are performed with alacrity. In relation to Abraham it is written (Bereishis 18:6), "And Abraham hastened to the tent, to Sarah, and he said, 'Hasten...' and he gave it to the youth and he hastened." And in relation to Rivkah (Ibid. 24:20), "And she hastened and emptied her pitcher... " And in the Midrash (Bamidbar Rabbah 10.17), " `And the woman made haste' (Judges 13:10) - this teaches us that all of the deeds of the righteous are done quickly," that they do not permit time to elapse before beginning them or in completing them.

The man whose soul burns in the service of his Creator will surely not idle in the performance of His mitzvos, but his movements will be like the quick movements of a fire; he will not rest or be still until the deed has been completed. Furthermore, just as zeal can result from an inner burning so can it create one. That is, one who perceives a quickening of his outer movements in the performance of a mitzvah conditions himself to experience a flaming inner movement, through which longing and desire will continually grow. If, however, he is sluggish in the movement of his limbs, the movement of his spirit will die down and be extinguished. Experience testifies to this.

It is known that what is most preferred in Divine service is desire of the heart and longing of the soul. And it is in relation to his goodly portion in this respect that David exulted (Tehillim 42:2), "As a hart yearns for the waterbrooks, so does my soul yearn for You, O Hashem. My soul thirsts for Hashem..." "My soul longs and goes out for the courts of Hashem (Tehillim 84:3); "My soul thirsts for You; my flesh pines for You" (Tehillim 63:2). The man in whom this longing does not burn as it should would do well to bestir himself by force of will so that, as a result, this longing will spring up in his nature; for outer movements awaken inner ones. Unquestionably a person has more control of his outer than of his inner self, but if he makes use of what he can control, he will acquire, in consequence, even that which is not within the province of his control. For as a result of the willed quickening of his movements, there will arise in him an inner joy and a desire and a longing. As the Prophet says (Hosea 6:3), "And let us know - let us run to know Hashem;" and (Hosea 11:10), "After Hashem will they go, who will roar like a lion."

CHAPTER VIII

CONCERNING THE MANNER OF ACQUIRING ZEAL

THE MEANS by which Zeal is acquired are the same as those by which Watchfulness is acquired, and their levels, too, are similar as I have written above; for their functions are very closely related and there is no distinct difference between them, except that one deals with positive, and the other with negative commandments. When a man realizes as a truth the great value of the mitzvos and the greatness of his responsibility in relation to them, his heart will certainly awaken to the service of Hashem and will not weaken in it. What may, however, strengthen this awakening is looking into all of the good things that Hashem does with a man at all periods and times, and into the great wonders that He does with him from the time of his birth until his last day. The more one looks into and considers these things, the more will he recognize his great debt to Hashem, who bestows good upon him, and he will be impelled not to grow lax or to weaken in His service. For since he cannot repay Hashem, he will feel that the least he can do is to exalt His Name and fulfill His mitzvos.

There is no man in any circumstances, poor or rich, healthy or ill, who cannot see wonders and many benefits in his condition. The rich and the healthy are indebted to Hashem for their riches and health respectively. The poor man is indebted to Him; for even in his poverty, Hashem miraculously and wondrously sustains him and does not permit him to die of hunger. The sick man is indebted to G- d because He strengthens him under the very weight of his illness and his wounds, and does not permit him to descend to the pit. And so with all other conditions. There is no man, then, who will not find himself indebted to the Creator. And when one regards the good things that he receives from Hashem, he will surely be awakened to Zealousness in His service, as I have written above, much more so if he considers the fact that all of his good depends upon Hashem and that his needs and necessities stem from Him, Hashem, and from no other - in which case he will certainly not be lax in his Divine service, in order not to lack what is essential to him.

You will note that I have embodied in my words the three categories which I discussed in relation to Watchfulness; for Zeal and Watchfulness are virtually the same, and what applies to one may be applied to the other. So that again, those with wholeness of understanding will be motivated by their sense of duty and by their appreciation of the value and worthiness of the deeds in question; those on a lower level, by their anxiety over the apportionment of honor in the World to Come and over the possibility of their being shamed on the day of reward by seeing what they could have had. but lost; and the populace in general, by their concern with this world and its needs, as heretofore explained.

CHAPTER IX

CONCERNING THE FACTORS WHICH DETRACT FROM ZEAL AND THE

WITHDRAWING OF ONESELF FROM THEM

THE FACTORS which detract from Zeal are those which promote laziness. The greatest of these is the desire for bodily repose - aversion to exertion - and the love of pleasures to their very limits. There is no question that a person laboring under the above deterrent will find Divine service a great burden. For one who wishes to take his meal with complete relaxation and repose, and to sleep without being disturbed and to walk only at a leisurely pace, and so forth - such a person will find it extremely difficult to arise for morning services or to curtail his dinner so as to pray the afternoon service before nightfall or to go out to perform a mitzvah if the time does not suit him. How much more reluctant will he be to rush himself for a mitzvah or for Torah study! One who habituates himself to these practices is not his own master to do the opposite of these things when he so desires, for his will is bound with the bonds of habit, which becomes second nature to him. A person must realize that he is not in this world for repose, but for labor and exertion. He should conduct himself according to the manner of laborers who work for hire (as it is said [Eruvin 65a], "We are day-laborers") and according to the manner of soldiers in the battle-line, who eat in haste, sleep only at irregular intervals and are always poised for attack. In relation to this it is said (Job 5:7), "A man is born to labor." If one accustoms himself to this approach, he will certainly find Divine service easy, for then he will not be lacking the proper attitude or preparation for it. Chazal said along the same lines (Avos 6.4), "This is the way of Torah - eat bread with salt, drink water by measure and sleep upon the ground." This regipeople constitutes the epitome of removal from comforts and pleasures.

Another deterrent to Zeal is trepidation and fear in relation to what time may bring, so that at one time one will be afraid of cold or heat, at another of accidents, at another of illnesses, at another of the wind, and so on and so forth. As was said by Solomon, may Peace be upon him (Mishlei 26:13), "The lazy man says, `There is a lion on the road, a lion between the ways.' " Chazal pointed up the degrading nature of this trait, attributing it to sinners. Scripture bears this out (Isaiah 33:14): "The sinners in Zion fear; a trembling has taken hold of the unHashemly." One of our great men, when he noticed one of his disciples in the grips of fear, said to him (Berachoth 60a), "You are a sinner." The proper rule of conduct is (Tehillim 37:3), "Trust in Hashem and do good; dwell in the land and cultivate faith."

In summary, a person should render himself rootless in the world and rooted in Divine service. In relation to all of the things of the world, he should be content with and able to get along with whatever comes his way; he should be far from repose and close to work and labor; his heart should trust securely in Hashem, and he should not fear the future and what it may bring.

If you will point to the fact that the Sages in all places have ordered that a man be especially attentive to his well-being and not put himself in danger even if he is righteous and a doer of good deeds, that they have said (Kethuvoth 30a), "All is in the hands of Heaven except chills and fever," and that the Torah states (Dvarim 4:15), "Be very watchful of your selves" - all of which indicates that a person is not to extend trust in Hashem to this area, even (as our Sages state further) when a mitzvah is to be performed - know that there is fear and there is fear. There is appropriate fear and there is foolish fear. There is confidence and there is recklessness. Hashem blessed be He, has invested man with sound intelligence and judgment so that he may follow the right path and protect himself from the instruments of injury that have been created to punish evildoers. One who allows himself not to be guided by wisdom and exposes himself to dangers is displaying not trust, but recklessness; and he is a sinner in that he flouts the will of the Creator, blessed be His Name, who desires that a man protect himself. Aside from the fact that because of his carelessness he lays himself open to the danger inherent in the threatening object, he openly calls punishment down upon himself because of the sin that he commits thereby, so that his hurt results from the sin itself.

The type of fear and self-protection which is appropriate is that which grows out of the workings of wisdom and intelligence. It is the type about which it is said (Mishlei 22:3), "The wise man sees evil and hides, but the fools pass on and are punished." "Foolish fear" is a person's desiring to multiply protection upon protection and fear upon fear, so that he makes a protection for his protection and neglects Torah and Divine service. The criterion by which to distinguish between the two fears is that implied in the statement of Chazal (Pesachim 8b), "Where there is a likelihood of danger, it is different." That is, where there is a recognized possibility of injury, one must be heedful, but where there is no apparent danger, one should not be afraid. Along the same lines it is said (Chullin 56b), "We do not assume an imperfection where we do not see one," and "A sage need be guided only by what his eyes see." (Bava Bathra 131 a). This is the very intent of the verse which we mentioned above: "The wise man sees the evil and hides..." What is spoken of is hiding from the evil which one sees, not from that which might, perhaps, possibly, materialize. And this is exactly the intent of the verse previously referred to:

"The lazy man says, `There is a lion on the road...,"' which Chazal interpreted (Devarim Rabbah 8:7) as an illustration of the extent to which vain fear can go to separate a man from a good deed: "Solomon said seven things in relation to the lazy man: If people say to the lazy man, `Your teacher is in the city; go and learn Torah from him,' he answers, `I am afraid of the lion on the road.' If they say, `Your teacher is within the province,' he answers, `I am afraid of the lion between the ways.' If they say, `He is in your house,' he answers, `If I go to him I will find the door locked..."' We see, then, that it is not fear which leads to laziness, but laziness which leads to fear.

All of what we have said is attested to by daily experience, in that to the vast majority of people it is obvious and well known that the type of attitude we have spoken of is that which fools are governed by. The perceptive person will recognize the truth of what has been said, and the man of understanding will readily acknowledge it.

The foregoing discussion of Zeal, I trust, will suffice to awaken the heart. He who is wise will wax wiser and add to his wisdom. Zeal, it should be noted, is appropriately placed a level above Watchfulness; for generally a person will not be Zealous unless he is first Watchful. One who does not concentrate upon being Watchful in his deeds and upon considering Divine service and its principles (such concentration constituting the trait of Watchfulness, as I have already written) will find it very difficult to cloak himself with love and yearning for it and to be Zealous with longing before His Creator; for such a person is still immersed in bodily desires and subject to the inclination of his habits, which draws him away from all this. However, after his eyes will have opened to see his deeds and to be Watchful of them, and he will have made the accounting of good deeds against bad that we mentioned, it will be easy for him to depart from evil and to long and be Zealous for good. This is self-evident.

CHAPTER X

CONCERNING THE TRAIT OF CLEANLINESS

THE IDEA behind the trait of Cleanliness is that a person be completely clean of bad traits and of sins, not only those which are recognized as such, but also those which are rationalized, which, when we look into them honestly, we find to be sanctioned only because of the heart's being still partially afflicted by lust and not entirely free of it, so as to incline us toward a relaxation of standards. The man who is entirely free of this affliction and clean of any trace of evil which lust leaves behind it will come to possess perfectly clean vision and pure discrimination, and will not be swayed in any direction by desire, but will recognize as evil, and withdraw from every sin that he had committed, though it were the slightest of the slight. Accordingly, Chazal referred to those individuals who so purified their deeds as to leave in them not even a stirring of evil as "the clean-minded people of Jerusalem" (Sanhedrin 23a).

You will now note the distinction between the Watchful and the Clean man (although they are closely related). The first is Watchful of his deeds and sees to it that he does not sin in relation to what he knows, and what is universally acknowledged to be sinful; however, he is still not so much master of himself as to keep his heart from being pulled along by natural lust and inclining him to rationalize in relation to things whose evil is not thus acknowledged. For even though he exerts himself to conquer his evil inclination and to subdue his desires, he will not, because of this, change his nature; he will not remove bodily lust from his heart. All he will be able to do is overcome it and be governed, not by it, but by reason. The darkness of earthiness, however, will still persist in its work of persuasion and deception. But when a person habituates himself to Watchfulness to the point where he completely cleanses himself of the acknowledged sins, and accustoms himself to zealous Divine service so that love and yearning for his Creator grow strong within him, then the force of this habituation will draw him farther from the realm of earthiness and direct his mind toward spiritual perfection. Eventually he will attain to perfect Cleanliness, a state in which physical desire is extinguished from his heart through the strengthening within him of the longing for Hashem. His vision will then possess the purity and clarity that I spoke of above. He will not be deceived, he will not be reached by the darkness of earthiness, and his deeds will be absolutely Clean.

David rejoiced in the possession of this trait and said (Tehillim 26:6), "I will wash my hands in Cleanliness and I will go around Your altar, O Hashem." In truth, it befits only him who is entirely clean of any stirring of sin or transgression to behold Hashem, the King; for lacking such cleanliness one should only be ashamed and disgraced before Him. As Ezra the Scribe said (Ezra 9:6), "My Hashem, I am ashamed and disgraced to lift, my Hashem, my face to You." Unquestionably the attainment of perfection in this trait entails great labor; for the recognized and well-known sins are easy to avoid since their evil is apparent, but the analysis which Cleanliness requires is of the most difficult kind, because the sin, involved, as I have written above, is hidden by rationalization. As Chazal have said Zarah 18a), "The sins which a man treads underfoot surround him at the time of judgment." And it was in this connection that they said (Bava Bathra 165a), "The majority succumb to the sin of theft, a minority to that of illicit relations and all of them to the `dust' of slander." The last, because of the extreme subtleness of its nature and its concomitant insusceptibility to recognition causes everyone to succumb to it.

Chazal tell us (Introduction to Eichah Rabbathi 30) that David was Watchful and Cleansed himself completely and that because of this he went to war with great confidence, asking (Tehillim 18:38), "Let me pursue my foes and overtake them; and let me not return until I have destroyed them," something which Yehoshafat, . Asa and Hezekiah, because they 1 ad not attained to such Cleanliness, did not ask. As David himself indicates within his statement (Ibid. 21), "Reward me, O Hashem, according to my righteousness; according to the Cleanliness of my hands repay me." And he says again (Ibid. 25), "Hashem rewarded me according to my righteousness, according to the Cleanliness of my hands before His eyes." David speaks here of the same kind of purity and Cleanliness that we have spoken of before. And he continues (Ibid. 30), "For with You will I run upon a troop." "I will pursue my foes and overtake them" (Ibid. 38). And he himself says again (Ibid. 24:3), "Who will ascend the mountain of Hashem, and who will stand in the place of His holiness? The Clean of hand and pure of heart."

This trait is certainly difficult to acquire, for a man's nature is weak. His heart is easily won over, and he permits certain things to himself by utilizing the opportunities for selfdeception which they present. One who has attained to the trait of Cleanliness has unquestionably reached a very high level of achievement, for he has stood up in the face of a raging battle and emerged victorious.

We shall now discuss the various particulars of this trait.

CHAPTER 11

CONCERNING THE PARTICULARS OF THE TRAIT OF CLEANLINESS

THE FACTORS which comprise Cleanliness are very numerous, being all of the factors which comprise the 365 negative commandments. For as I have already stated, the objective of this trait is to be clean of all of the forms of sin. However, though the evil inclination causes a man to commit all kinds of sins, there are some which a person's nature renders more desirable to him, and, consequently, provides him with more rationalizations for. He therefore requires in relation to them additional strengthening to vanquish his evil inclination and be clean of sin. In this connection Chazal have said (Chagigah I lb), "There is within a person a desire and a longing for theft and illicit relations." Although we see that most people are not manifest thieves in the sense of openly confiscating their neighbors' belongings and depositing them among their own possessions, most of them get the taste of theft in the course of their business dealings by allowing themselves to gain through their neighbors' loss, saying, "Business is different."

Many prohibitions, however, were stated in regard to theft: "Do not steal," "Do not rob," "Do not oppress," "And you shall not deny," "And a man should not speak falsely against his neighbor," "A man should not deceive his brother," "Do not push back your neighbor's boundary." These varied laws of theft take in many of the most common types of transactions, in relation to all of which there are many prohibitions. For it is not the overt, acknowledged deed of oppression or theft alone which is forbidden; but anything which would lead to such a deed and bring it about is included in the prohibition. Concerning this Chazal said (Sanhedrin 8 la), "`And he did not pollute his neighbor's wife' (Ezekiel 18:15) - he did not infringe upon his neighbor's occupation." R. Yehudah forbade a storekeeper to distribute roasted grain and nuts to children to accustom them to come to him; the other Sages permitted it only because his competitor could do the same (Bava Metzia 60a). Chazal have also said (Bava Bathra 88b), "Stealing from a person is worse than stealing from Hashem, for concerning the first, the fact of one's being a sinner is stated before that of his having committed a wrong ..." They also exempted hired workers from the blessing over bread and from the latter blessings of Grace. And even in the case of the Shema they required them to leave off working only for the recitation of the first section (Berachoth 16b) . How obvious is it, then, that a day -laborer has no right to interrupt the work assigned to him for mundane considerations, and that if he does, he is a thief. Abba Chilkiyah did not even return the greeting of Scholars so that he would not interrupt the work he was doing for his neighbor (Ta'anith 23b). And our father Jacob, may Peace be upon him, explicitly stated (Bereishis 31:40), "In the daytime I was consumed by drought and in the evening by frost, and my sleep fled from my eyes." What, then, will those say who occupy themselves with their pleasures and leave off working, or those who during their working-time engage in their own affairs for personal gain?

In fine, if one is hired by his neighbor for any kind of labor, all of his hours are sold to his employer for the day. As Chazal say (Bava Metzia 56b), "Hiring oneself out is equivalent to selling oneself for the day." Any utilization of these hours for his personal benefit in any manner whatsoever is gross theft, and if his employer does not forgive him, he is not forgiven. As our Teachers of blessed memory have said (Yoma 85b), "The Day of Atonement does not atone for a man's sins against his neighbor until he pacifies him." What is more, even if one performs a mitzvah during his working -time, he is not credited with righteousness, but charged with a transgression. A transgression cannot be a mitzvah. It is written (Isaiah 61:8), "I hate theft in a burnt -offering." Along the same lines Chazal have said (Bava Kamma 94a), "One who steals a measure of wheat, grinds it, bakes it and pronounces a blessing over it, is not blessing, but abusing, as it is written (Tehillim 10:3), `And the thief who blesses, abuses Hashem.' " Similarly it is said, "Woe unto him whose defense attorney becomes his prosecutor." This is analogous to what our Sages say (Yerushalmi Sukkah 3.1) concerning a stolen lulav. Stealing an object is stealing, and stealing time is stealing. As with a stolen object that is used for a mitzvah, so with stolen time that is similarly used, one's defense attorney becomes his prosecutor.

Hashem desires only honesty, as it is said (Tehillim 31:24), "Hashem protects the honest ones," and (Isaiah 26:2), "Open ye doors so that there may enter a righteous nation, a keeper of trusts," and (Tehillim 101:6), "My eyes are to the trusted people of the earth, that they may sit with me," and (Jeremiah 5:3), "Are Your eyes not to faithfulness?" Even Job said about himself (Job 31:7), "Did my steps deviate from the path? Did my eyes follow my heart? Did anything adhere to my palm?" Regard the beauty of this comparison in which concealed theft is likened to a thing which sticks to a person's hand. Though he had no original intention of taking it, the fact remains that it is in his hand. Here, too, though a man does not actually go out and steal, it is difficult for his hands to be entirely clean of theft, for the eyes instead of being ruled by the heart so that they do not find pleasing to them what belongs to others, pull the heart after them to seek rationalizations for the acquisition of what seems beautiful and desirable to them. Job tells us, in effect, that he did not conduct himself in this manner, that his heart did not follow his eyes, and that, therefore, nothing stuck to his palm.

Consider the question of deceit. How easy it is for a person to deceive himself and fall prey to sin. On the surface it seems proper to him to attempt to make his wares attractive to people and to profit by his efforts, as it does to use "sales talk" on the prospective purchaser to render him more receptive; especially so in the face of such popular encomiums as "The quick man profits" (Pesachim 506) and "The hand of the diligent prospers" (Mishlei 10:4). But if he does not analyze and weigh his actions carefully, he will bring forth thorns instead of wheat, for he will transgress and fall victim to the sin of deceit about which we have been warned, (Leviticus 25:17), "Let not a man deceive his fellow." Chazal have said (Chullin 94a) that it is forbidden also to fool a non-Jew. It is written (Zephaniah 3:13), "The remnant of Israel will not do iniquity and they will not speak falsehood, and a deceiving tongue will not be found in their mouths." Our Sages have said (Bava Metzia 60a), "It is forbidden to paint old vessels to give them the appearance of new ones. It is forbidden to mix the fruits of one field with those of another, though the latter be just as fresh as the first, and though they be worth a dinar and a tresis per measure, and the combination be sold for only a dinar per measure." "All who do these, all doers of wrong" (Dvarim 25:16). Five designations have been applied to them: "wrong," "hateful," "abominable," "despised," "detested." (Sijra 19.35). Chazal have further stated (Bava Kamma 119a), "If one steals even the worth of a prutah from his neighbor, it is as if he takes his soul from him." This statement reveals to us the severity of this sin even where a trifling amount is involved. And they said again (Ta'anith 7b), "The rains are held back only because of the sin of theft," and again, (Vayikra Rabbah 33.3), "in a basketful of sins, which is the most incriminating?- theft." The doom of the generation of the flood was sealed only because of the sin of theft (Sanhedrin 108a).

If you ask yourself, "How is it possible for us in our dealings not to attempt to favorably incline the prospective buyer toward the object to be sold and its worth?" know that there is a great distinction to be made. Whatever effort is made to show the purchaser the true worth and beauty of the object is fitting and proper, but whatever is done to conceal its imperfections constitutes deceit and is forbidden. This is an elemental principle in business honesty. And this goes without saying in respect to malpractice in the area of weights and measures, in relation to which it is explicitly written (Dvarim 25:16) : "The abomination of Hashem, your Hashem, are all who do these." Chazal have said (Bava Bathra 88b), "The punishment for dishonest weights and measures is more severe than that for illicit relations ..." (Ibid. a), and "The wholesale merchant must clean his measures once in thirty days." Why must this be done? So that the purchasers not unknowingly get less than what they paid for and the merchant not be punished.

What we have said, naturally applies to the sin of taking interest, which is as great a sin as denying the Hashem of Israel, Hashem forbid (Bava Metzia 71a). Chazal said (Shemoth Rabbah 31.6) in relation to the verse (Ezekiel 18:13), "He gave with usury and took interest, and shall he live? He shall not live," that he who takes interest will not experience the revival of the dead, for he and his dust are abominable and detestable in the eyes of Hashem. I see no need to expatiate on this sin, for its fearful nature is felt by every Jew.

In fine, just as the desire for acquisition is great, so are there many pitfalls which it presents; and for a person to be completely Clean of them, there must be great scrutiny and much analysis on his part. If he does cleanse himself of this desire, let him know that he has reached a very high level of achievement; for there are many who achieve saintliness in many areas, but who cannot achieve perfection in despising dishonest gain. As Tzofar the Naamasite said to Job (Job 11:14), "If there is wickedness in your hand put it far from yourself, and do not permit wrong to dwell in your tents; for then you will lift up your face from imperfection and you will be strong and not fear."

I have spoken thus far of the particulars of one of the mitzvos. There is no question that each and every mitzvah lends itself to such analysis. I am discussing only those, however, which most people are generally remiss in.

We shall now consider the sin of illicit relations, which is also included among the most severe sins, being second only to theft, as revealed in the statement of Chazal (Bava Bathra 165a), "The majority succumb to the sin of theft, a minority to that of illicit relations." One who desires to be completely clean of this sin also requires no little effort, for its prohibition takes in not only the act itself, but anything that approaches it, as Scripture clearly states (Leviticus 18:6), "Do not come near to uncover nakedness." And Chazal have said (Shemoth Rabbah 16:2), "Hashem said, `Do not say, "Since I may not live with a woman, I will hold her and be free of sin, I will embrace her and be free of sin; or I will kiss her and be free of sin." ' Hashem said, `Just as when a Nazarite takes a vow not to drink wine, he is forbidden to eat grapes or raisins or drink grape juice, or partake of anything, for that matter, which comes from the grapevine, so is it forbidden to touch any woman but your own wife; and anyone who does touch a woman other than his wife brings death to himself.' " See how wonderful these words are! The prohibition in the case of illicit relations is likened to that in the case of a Nazarite, where, even though the essence of the prohibition involves only the drinking of wine, the Torah forbids to him anything which has some connection with wine. Through what it says concerning a Nazarite, the Torah is teaching the Sages hjw to make "a fence around the Torah" by way of implementing the authority vested in them to reinforce the Torah's rulings. Using the case of the Nazarite as a prototype, the Torah is instructing the Sages to proscribe, because of a basic prohibition, anything that is similar to it. To reveal Hashem's will in the matter, the Torah did in relation to the mitzvah of the Nazarite what it authorized the Sages to do in relation to all the other mitzvos, namely, to forbid anything which approaches the nature of what is proscribed, by deducing what is not stated from what is stated. By applying this principle to the area of illicit relations, the Sages prohibited anything partaking of the nature of fornication or approaching it, regardless of the particular avenue of approach, whether that of deed, or sight, or speech, or hearing, or even thought.

I will now substantiate what has been said by referring to the words of Chazal

Deed : Namely touching or embracing and the like. This has already been considered in the aforementioned statement and there is no need to dwell upon it.

Sight : Chazal have said (Berachoth 61a), " ` Hand to hand, the evil will not be cleansed' (Mishlei 11:21) - one who counts coins from his hand to hers in order to gaze at her will not be cleansed from the judgment of Gehinnom." And again (Shabbath 64a), "Why did the Jews of that generation require atonement?- because they fed their eyes on impurity." R. Shesheth said (Berachoth 24a), "Why did Scripture (Numbers 31:50) enumerate the outer ornaments together with the inner ones?- to teach us that if one gazes at a woman's little finger, it is as if he gazed at her impurity." And again (Avodah Zarah 20a), " `And keep yourself from every evil thing' (Dvarim 23:10) - a man should not eye a beautiful woman, even if she is unmarried, and a married woman, even if she is ugly."

Speech : It is explicitly stated (Avos 1.5), "One who converses at length with a woman draws evil upon himself."

Hearing : (Berachoth 24a), "A woman's singing is impurity."

Concerning the "fornication of the mouth and the ear," that is, speaking obscenities or listening to them, our Sages "screamed like cranes" (Yerushalmi Terumoth 1.4), " `Let there not be seen within you a thing of nakedness' (Dvarim 23:15) - nakedness of speech, the uttering of obscenities." And (Shabbath 33a), "Because of the sin of obscene speech, troubles renew themselves and the youths of Israel die, G- d forbid." And (Ibid.), "If one sullies his mouth, Gehinnom is deepened for him." And (Ibid.), "Everyone knows why a bride goes to the wedding canopy, but anyone who speaks obscenely concerning it, even a decree of seventy good years is converted to evil." And (Chagigah 5b), "Even a casual conversation between a man and his wife is held up to him at the time of Judgment." And concerning listening to obscenities they said (Shabbath 33a),` `Even one who listens and remains still, as it is said (Mishlei 22:14), `He who has incurred Hashem's wrath, shall fall therein.' " We see, then, that all of one's faculties must be Clean of fornication and of anything related to it.

If one would gain your ear and tell you that the Sages said what they did in relation to obscene speech only to frighten one and to draw him far from sin, and that their words apply only to hot-blooded individuals who, by speaking obscenities, would be aroused to lust, but not to those who air them only in jest, in which case there is nothing whatever to fear- tell him that his words are those of the evil inclination; for the Sages have adduced an explicit verse in support of their statements (Isaiah 9:16): "Therefore Hashem will not rejoice over their youths ... for they are all flatterers and speakers of evil, and every mouth utters obscentities." This verse mentions neither idol worship, nor illicit relations, nor murder, but flattery and slander and obscene utterance, all sins of the mouth in its capacity of speech; and it is because of these sins that the decree went forth, "Therefore Hashem will not rejoice over their youths, and will not be merciful to their orphans and widows ..." The truth, then, is as our Teachers of blessed memory have it, that the uttering of obscenities is the very "nakedness" of the faculty of speech and was prohibited as an aspect of fornication along with all other such aspects, which, although outside the realm of the act of illicit relations itself (as indicated by their not being subject to the punishment of "cutting off" or to the death penalty), are nonetheless prohibited in themselves; this aside from the fact that they also conduce to and bring about the principally proscribed act itself, as in the case of the Nazarite in the Midrash referred to above. Thought: Chazal have already said in the beginning of our Baraitha (Avodah Zarah 20b), " `And keep yourself from every evil thing' (Dvarim 23:10)-a man should not think obscene thoughts in the daytime ... " And (Yoma 29a), "The thoughts behind the sin are worse than the sin itself." And Scripture explicitly states (Mishlei 15:26), "Evil thoughts are the abomination of Hashem."

We have spoken thus far of two severe types of sin whose various forms are likely be stumbling blocks both because of the innumerability of these forms and because of the strong lustful inclination of a person's heart in relation to them.

The sin which comes third after theft and illicit relations in respect to desire is that of forbidden foods - whether thos; that are ritually unclean, or an admixture containing them, or a combination of meat and milk, or suet, or blood, or food cooked by gentiles, or the utensils of gentiles, or the wine used in ther libations, or their drinking-wine. Cleanliness in relation to all of these requires great scrutiny and self-strengthening because there is a lust in the heart for good foods and because one must sometimes suffer a monetary loss as a result of admixtures and the like. The prohibitions concerning forbidden foods also involve many details, as is reflected in all of the commonly known laws that are treated in the Halachic writings. One who is lenient in relation to these laws when he has been instructed to be stringent is destroying his soul. As is stated in the Sifra (Shemini), " `Do not sully yourselves with them, becoming unclean with them' (Leviticus 11:43) - if you sully yourselves with them, you will, in the end, partake of their uncleanliness." Forbidden foods carry uncleanliness itself into a person's heart and soul until the holiness of the Presence Blessed be He departs and withdraws from him, as is also stated in the Talmud (Yoma 39a), " `...becoming unclean with them' - do not read `becoming unclean with them,' but `becoming dull with them.' " For sin dulls a man's heart in that it causes to depart from him true knowledge and the spirit of wisdom that Hashem gives to the Tzaddikim (as it is said [Mishlei 2:6], "For Hashem gives wisdom"), and he remains beastly and earthy, immersed in the grossness of this world. Forbidden foods are worse in this respect than all other prohibitions, for they enter into a person's body and become flesh of his flesh. In order to instruct us that this applies not only to unclean beasts or to earth creatures, but also to those animals, which, though in the "clean" category, are ritually unclean, Scripture tells us (Leviticus 11:47), "To distinguish between the unclean and the clean," upon which our Teachers of blessed memory comment (Sifra ad loc.), "There is no need to point up the distinction between an ass and a cow. What, then, is the meaning of `between the unclean and the clean'? - between what is unclean to you and what is clean to you; between the cutting of most of the windpipe and the cutting of half. And what is the difference between most and half ? - a hairs -breadth." The reason that they concluded in this manner ("And what is the difference between `most' ... ") is to show how amazing the power of the mitzvos is, that a hair's-breadth constitutes the difference between uncleanliness and cleanliness itself.

Anyone possessed of sense will regard forbidden food as poison, or as food with which some poison has become mixed. Would anyone allow himself to partake of such food? If there were any room for suspicion or even the slightest doubt, he would certainly not permit himself to eat of it; and if he did, he would be regarded as an absolute fool. Forbidden food, as we have explained, is poison itself to the heart and soul. Who, then, possessing any intelligence, would allow himself to eat food about whose permissibility there is some question? Concerning this it is said (Mishlei 23:2), "And put a knife to your throat if you have any sense."

We shall now discuss the common sins which grow out of the relationships between people and their association in groups. Among these are: verbal oppression, shaming, giving misleading advice, tale -bearing, hating, taking revenge, taking oaths, lying, and desecrating the Name. Who can say, "I am Clean of them; I am pure of any fault in respect to them"? Their various aspects are so numerous and subtle that Watchfulness in relation to them is extremely burdensome.

Included in the sin of verbal oppression is shaming one's neighbor by words in private; much more so, shaming him thus in public or doing something to him which causes him to be ashamed in public. As stated in Perek Hazahav (Bava Metzia 58b), "If he has repented, one should not say to him, `Remember your former deeds ...' If he is beset by sickness, one should not say to him as was said to Job by his friends (Job 4:7), `Remember, which clean man is destroyed ... ? ' If donkey-drivers ask grain of him, let him not say to them, `Go to so and so, for he sells grain, ' knowing full well that he never sold grain in his whole life." Chazal have stated (Bava Metzia 58b), "Verbal oppression is worse than monetary oppression [deceit] ..." This is especially true as regards shaming one in public, for we were explicitly taught (Avos 3.11), "One who shames his neighbor in public has no share in the World to Come." R. Chisda said (Bava Metzia 59a), "All of the gates of prayer were closed except those through which pass the cries of those who have been oppressed by words." And R. Eleazar said (Ibid.), "Hashem exacts payment through a messenger for every sin, except that of verbal oppression." Our Sages said (Ibid.), "There are three sins which the curtain does not block out." One of those mentioned is the sin of verbal oppression. Even in the case of the observance of mitzvos, in relation to which Scripture tells us (Leviticus 19:17), "But you shall rebuke your friend, " Chazal say (Arachin 16b), "i would think that this applies even to the extent of causing his face to change color; therefore, we are told immediately afterwards, `But do not bear a sin because of it.' " All of these statements reveal to us how far the warning against the sin of verbal oppression branches out and how severe its punishment is.

Concerning the giving of misleading advice we learned in Torath Kohanim (Leviticus 19:14), " `And do not place a stumbling block before a blind man' - before one who is blind to something. If you are asked whether someone's daughter may marry a Kohen, do not answer affirmatively if you know the opposite to be the case. If someone asks you for advice, do not give advice which is not suitable for him ... And do not say to him, `Sell your field and buy an ass,' by way attempting to gain possession of the field for yourself. You might say to yourself, `I am giving him a good piece of advice,' but your heart knows the truth, as it is stated (Ibid), `And fear your Hashem."'

We see, then, that when one is approached for advice, his counsel, whether there is a possibility of his being personally affected by it or not, must be in accordance with pure, clear truth. Observe that the Torah has penetrated into the very recesses of the deceiver's mind, for we are speaking here not of coarse men, who openly give advice that is obviously malicious, but of those who are skilled in evil, whose advice, on the surface, seems truly to be to their friend's interest, but which, in reality, is not for his good, but to his detriment and for their own benefit. It is in this connection that we were told, "You might say to yourself, `I am giving him a good piece of advice,' but your heart knows the truth..." To what a profound extent do people succumb to these sins every day in responding to the powerful call of desire for gain! Scripture reveals the terrible nature of the punishment in this case (Dvarim 27:18): "Accursed is he who misleads a blind man on the path."

This is the duty of the just man: When someone requests his advice, he should tell him to do what he himself would do in a similar situation, having no other end, immediate or distant, than the good of the one he is advising. And if it so happens that he sees himself as standing to lose through such advice, if he is in a position to reveal the same to the other, he should do so and if not he should excuse himself and give no advice whatsoever. In any event however, he must not propose anything whose end is not the good of the person seeking advice, unless the latter intends evil, in which case it is certainly a mitzvah to deceive him, as it is said (Tehillim 18:27), "And with the crooked be cunning." The episode of Chushai the Archite (11 Samuel 15:32 ff) is a case in point.

The severity of tale-bearing and slander is already known, as is also the profusion of forms that it assumes. It is, moreover, such a great profusion, that Chazal pronounced, in a statement that I have already referred to, (Bava Bathra 165a), " And all of them succumb to the `dust' of slander." They ask (Arachin 15b), "What is the dust of slander?" and answer, "One's saying, `Where is a hearth-fire found? Only in so and so's house,' " or one's praising his neighbor in the presence of the latter's enemies, and the like. Even though such things may appear very insignificant and very far removed from tale-bearing, they are, in truth, part of its "dust."

In fine, the evil inclination has many devices at its command. Any statement that a man makes concerning his neighbor, in his presence or not, which might cause him injury or shame is included in the sin of slander, which is hated and despised by the Presence, and about which it is said (Ibid.),

"If one utters slanderous remarks it is as if he denies the First Cause," and (Tehillim 101:5), "One who slanders his friend in secret, him will I destroy. "

Hate and revenge, too, are very difficult for man's spiteful heart to escape, for in view of his being extremely sensitive to insult, and suffering great anguish because of it, revenge, being the only thing which will put him at rest, is sweeter than honey to him. Therefore, if it is within his power to abandon the urging of his nature and to overlook the offense so as not to hate the one who ignited hatred within him, nor to take revenge against him when the opportunity to do so presents itself, nor to hold a grudge against him, but to forget the whole affair and remove it from his heart as if it had never occurred - if he can do this, he is strong and courageous. Such conduct is easy only for the ministering angels among whom the aforementioned traits do not exist, not for "dwellers in houses of clay whose roots are in dust" (Job 4:19). But the King has decreed (in perfectly lucid language, requiring no interpretation) (Leviticus 19:17,18), "Do not hate your brother in your heart ... Do not take revenge and do not bear a grudge against the children of your nation."

The difference between taking revenge and bearing a grudge is that the first indicates a person's withholding good from one who kept some good from him or injured him in some way, whereas the second denotes a person's interlarding a worthy act toward one who had wronged him with some reminder of that wrong.

The evil inclination advances and inflames the heart and constantly seeks to leave at least some trace or memory of the wrong. If it is not successful in leaving a strong reminder it will attempt to leave a weaker one. For example, it will tell a person, "If you wish to give this man what he did not want to give you when you were in need, at least do not give it to him graciously." Or, "If you do not want to hurt him, at least do not do him a great favor or offer him valuable assistance." Or, "If you want to go so far as to be of great help to him, at least do not provide this help in his presence." Or, "If you have forgiven him, do not renew your acquaintance with him and become his friend; it is enough that you do not show yourself his enemy. And if you want to go so far as to befriend him, at least do not show him as much friendship as of yore."

All such suggestions are among the intrigues of the evil inclination, by which it attempts to ensnare a person's heart. To counteract this the Torah states a general, all-embracing principle (Ibid.): "And love your friend as yourself" - "as yourself," with no difference whatsoever - "as yourself," without distinction, without devices and schemes - literally "as yourself."

As far as oaths are concerned, even though all those who are not of the common run of people guard themselves from taking the name of Hashem in vain, especially in oaths, there are still some small offshoots of this sin which, although not among the most severe transgressions, should nevertheless be avoided by those who wish to be Clean. As has been stated (Shevuoth 36a), "R. Eleazar said, 'No' is an oath and `Yes' is an oath. Rava said, `Only if one said 'No, No'- twice or `Yes, Yes' -- twice.' " And, (Bava Metzia 49a), " `A righteous measure' (Leviticus 19:36) - your `No' should be righteous and your `Yes' should be righteous."

Lying, too, is a terrible sickness that has spread far-reachingly among men. There are various levels of this sin.

There are some people whose profession itself is lying, who go around inventing stark falsehoods in order to promote social intercourse or to be reckoned among the wise and informed. In relation to them it is said (Mishlei 12:22), "The abomination of Hashem is lying lips," and (Isaiah 59:3), "Your lips speak falsehood, your tongues give voice to wrong."

And Chazal have pronounced their judgment (Sotah 42a), "There are four classes of people who are not received into the presence of Hashem." (The class of liars is numbered among the four).

There are other liars close to the first kind in regard to level, although not exactly like them; namely, those who lie within their stories and their statements. That is, it is not their practice to go around inventing stories and manufacturing incidents which never occurred, but, when they give an account of something, they interlard it with falsehoods as their fancy strikes them. They habituate themselves to this practice to the point where it becomes part of their nature. These are the liars whose words it is impossible to believe, as stated by Chazal (Sanhedrin 89b), "This is the punishment of a liar - even when he speaks truth he is not attended to." They have implanted this evil so deeply within themselves that their words cannot leave their lips clean of falsehood. As the Prophet grieves (Jeremiah 9:4), "They have taught their tongues to speak falsehood; they have become weary with wrong."

There are others whose sickness is milder than that of the first two types. The members of this third group are not confirmed in falsehood, but do not take heed to withdraw from it, and speak it when the opportunity presents itself, and very often by way of jest and the like, with no evil intent. The Sage, however, has made it known to us that all of this is contrary to the will of the Creator, blessed be He, and to the attribute of His Tzaddikim (Mishlei 13:5): "The righteous hate a false thing." And it is in relation to this that we were warned (Exodus 23:7), "Withdraw from a false thing." Note that we do not have, "Guard yourself from falsehood," but "Withdraw from a false thing," this to awaken us to the greatness of the extent to which one must withdraw himself and flee from falsehood. As has been stated (Zechariah 3:13), "The remnant of Israel will not do wrong and will not speak falsehood; and a deceiving tongue will not be found in their mouths." Chazal have said (Shabbath 55a), "The seal of Hashem is truth." Indeed if the truth is what Hashem selected as His seal, how abominable must its opposite be to Him. Hashem furnished us with a great exhortation concerning the necessity of abiding by the truth (Zechariah 8:16), "Let one man speak with another in truth; " and (Isaiah 16:5), "And a throne will be established in loving-kindness and He will sit upon it in Truth;" and (Ibid. 63:8), "And He said, `But they are my people, children who do not lie;' " (one is dependent upon the other) and (Zechariah 8:3), "And Jerusalem will be called "The City of Truth" (this to magnify its worth). And Chazal have said (Makkoth 24a), " `And he speaks the truth in his heart' (Tehillim 15:2), as R. Safra..." [Rashi explains: "This is the incident concerning R. Safra: he had a certain article to sell, but when someone approached him while he was reciting the Shema, and said to him, `Give me the article for so much and so much money,' he did not answer, being occupied in the recitation of the Shema. The latter, thinking that he did not want to give him the object for that sum, continued, `Give it to me for so much and so much more.' After completing the Shema, he said to him, `Take the article for the sum you originally stipulated, for I had intended to give it to you for that sum.' "] This to show how far one is duty-bound to be truthful. They have forbidden (Bava Metzia 23b), a Scholar to alter his language except for three things.

Truth is one of the pillars upon which the world stands (Avos 1.18). Speaking falsehood, then, is comparable to removing the foundation of the world; and, conversely, if one is heedful of the truth it is as if he maintains the world's foundation. Chazal told us (Sanhedrin 97a) of a community which was watchful of truth and in which the Angel of Death was powerless; but because the wife of a certain teacher altered her language, cven though her intentions were good, the Angel of Death was loosed upon it. After she had been driven away because of this, the old serenity returned. There is no need to dwell further upon this because it is dictated by intelligence and borne out by reason.

The aspects of "desecration of the Name" are also numerous and significant, for a person must be extremely jealous of his Master's honor, and subject everything he does to great scrutiny and thought in order that it not give rise to what might possibly be a desecration of the Name of Heaven, Hashem forbid. We have learned (Avos 4.4), "The sin of desecration of the Name obtains both in the presence and in the absence of intent." And Chazal have said (Yoma 86a), "What constitutes desecration of the Name? Rav said, `If one such as I were to buy meat without paying for it immediately,' and R. Yochanan said, `If one such as I were to walk four ells without Torah and tefillin.' " The idea behind this is that every man, according to the level that he is on and according to the impression that people have of him must engage in thought in order to keep himself from doing anything not befitting a man such as he. To the extent of his importance and wisdom, he should cultivate his Watchfulness in matters of Divine service and deepen his consideration of it. And if he does not do so, the Name of Heaven is desecrated through him, Hashem forbid. For it is to the honor of the Torah that one who learns more of it progresses more, likewise, in righteousness and in refinement of character traits. Any lack in this respect, on the part of one who learns a great deal, contributes to a disparagement of learning itself, which is, Hashem forbid, a desecration of the Name of Hashem, who gave us His holy Torah and commanded us to occupy ourselves with it in order to attain our perfection.

The observance of Sabbaths and Festivals is also of especially great significance, for their laws are very numerous. As it is said (Shabbath 12a), "There are many laws in relation to the Sabbath." Even the laws of "resting," Rabbinical ordinances, are essential principles; as it is said (Chagigah 16b), "The principle of `resting' should not be taken lightly, for the prohibition against semichah is an aspect of `resting' and the great people of the generation contended over it." The details of the laws of the Sabbath, according to their divisions are explained in the Halachic writings. They are all equal in respect to our duty concerning them and in respect to the degree of Watchfulness required. The difficult part of Sabbath observance for most people is abstaining from occupation and from discussion of business activities, the prohibition against which is stated in the words of the Prophet (Isaiah 58:13), "And honor it by abstaining from ordering your ways, from fulfilling your desires and from engaging in speech." The rule is that everything which may not be done on the Sabbath may not be striven after or mentioned. It was for these reasons that Chazal forbade a man to survey his property to see what it might require the next day, or to walk to the gates of the province in order to be able to depart on a long journey soon after nightfall, or to say, "i will do such and such tomorrow," or "I will buy such and such wares tomorrow," and the like.

I have thus far spoken of those few mitzvos which we see people to be most remiss in. What we have said about these should serve us for all the other prohibitions, for there is no prohibition without divisions and particulars, some more severe, some less. One who wishes to be Clean must be clean and pure in all of them. Chazal have said (Shir Hashirim Rabbah 6.12), " `Your teeth are like a flock of sheep' (Canticles 6:6) - just as a sheep is modest in its behavior so were the Jews modest and virtuous in the war with Midian. R. Huna said in the name of R. Acha, `During the war with Midian, not one of them put on the tefillin of the head before the tefillin of the hand. If one of them had done so, Moshe would not have praised them and they would not have left the field in peace.' " As stated in Yerushalmi, "One who speaks between Yishtabach and Yotzer is tainted with a transgression and must leave the battle-field because of it."

We see, then, the extent to which analysis and true Cleanliness are necessary in relation to deeds. But just as Cleanliness must reside in deeds, so must it reside in traits. In fact, it is almost more difficult to acquire the second type of Cleanliness than the first, for one's nature is more influential in the sphere of his traits than in that of his deeds, in that one's temperament and character can be a great help or a great hindrance in the formation of his traits. And every struggle against one's nature is a fierce one, as Chazal have stated (Avos 4.1), "Who is strong? One who conquers his evil inclination."

There are innumerable traits; for as all of a person's worldly actions, so are his traits. It is from them that his actions flow. But just as we discussed those mitzvos which there was a greater need to consider, because of the greater frequency of lapses in relation to them, so shall we discuss the chief traits in greater detail because of the relative frequency with which they come into play. These are pride, anger, envy, and lust - all evil traits, whose evil is widely recognized and need not be demonstrated. They are evil both in themselves and in their results, for they are all outside the realm of intelligence and wisdom. Each one of them has it within itself to lead a person into severe sins. In relation to pride we are explicitly warned (Dvarim 8:14), "And your heart will be proud and you will forget Hashem, your Hashem." Concerning anger Chazal said (Shabbath 1056), "One who becomes angry should be in your eyes as one who serves idols." About envy and lust we were told explicitly (Avos 4.21), "Envy, lust and honor-seeking remove one from the world." The necessary insight in relation to them is to flee all of them and all that derives from them, for they are all as one, "deviant offshoots of a strange vine" (Jeremiah 2:21). We shall now proceed to discuss them individually.

Pride consists in a person's pluming himself with his self and considering himself worthy of praise. There can be many different reasons behind this. Some deem themselves intelligent; some, handsome; some, honored; some, great; some, wise. In fine, when a man attributes to himself any of the good things of the world, he puts himself in immediate danger of falling into the pit of pride. However, a person's convincing himself of his significance and of his meriting praise leads not to one result only, but to many different results. It is even possible for opposing reactions to stem from similar causes and to be directed to the same end.

One type of pride reflects itself in a person's thinking that since he is deserving of praise and is impressively unique (as he imagines) in the possession of his particular attribute, he should deport himself, too, in a manner that is impressively unique, highly dignified, in walking, sitting, rising, speaking in all of his actions. He will walk only in an unhurried manner, with measured step; he will sit only erect; he will rise only little by little, like a snake; he will not speak with all people, but only with people of eminence; and even with them, he will utter only terse, oracular remarks. And in all of his other actions -- his movements, his manipulations, his eating, his drinking, his dressing, and in all of his ways - he will conduct himself with great pompousness, as if all of his flesh were lead and all of his bones, stone or earth.

Another type of pride manifests itself in a man's thinking that since he is worthy of praise and possessed of many superior qualities he must become the terror of the earth and everyone must tremble before him. He feels that it would be insolent on the part of people to speak with him or to ask anything of him. If they dare to approach him, he will confound them with his voice and drive them into a turmoil with the breath of his lips, with his biting retorts. And his face will continuously fume.

A third type of pride reveals itself in one's thinking that he is already so great and so invested with honor that honor is inseparable from him and that, consequently, he need not pursue it. To impress this upon others, he fashions his deeds after those of humble people and goes to very great lengths to exhibit [Variant: calls attention to his character, exhibiting] unusual and unfathomable humility, his heart all the time swelling within him, as if to say, "I am so exalted and so greatly honored that I no longer have any need for honor and might just as well decline it, for it resides with me in great measure."

Yet another type of pride expresses itself in a person's desiring to be widely renowned for his outstanding qualities and for the uniqueness of his ways, to the point where it is not enough for him to be praised by all the world for the qualities he imagines himself to possess, but he desires to be praised even more for being the humblest of the humble. Such a one prides himself upon his humility and desires honor because he shows himself to flee it. He puts himself beneath those who are far inferior to him, or beneath the derelicts of society, seeking to display thereby the essence of humility. He shuns all imposing titles and refuses all dignities, his heart all the while saying within him, "There is no wiser and humbler man than I in all the land." Those who possess this type of pride, though they give the impression of humility, face no few pitfalls, for without their being aware of it, their pride will be revealed, as a flame escaping from shards. Chazal have already compared (Bamidbar Rabbah 18.13) a person with this kind of pride to a house full of straw. The straw enters into cracks in the walls, and, after a few days, begins to emerge, so that everyone realizes the house is full of it. Similarly, those people who possess this type of pride will not always be able to conceal their true identity. Their evil intent will show through their deeds and their seeming self-effacement will be recognized as specious humility and deceitful lowliness.

There are others whose pride remains buried in their hearts without receiving expression in deed, but who nurse the thought that they are great sages who know things to their very depths, and that not many can hope to be as wise as they. And so thinking, they pay no heed to the thoughts of others, reasoning that what they cannot comprehend no one can.What is dictated to them by their intelligence is so clear and obvious to them that they cannot even consider any arguments to the contrary, regardless of the stature of those who put them forward. They have no doubts whatsoever as to the correctness of their views.

All of these reactions stem from pride, which sets back sages and stultifies their minds, which perverts the hearts of the highest in wisdom. And even raw students whose eyes have barely opened, are caused by pride to fancy themselves the wisest of the wise. Concerning all forms of pride it is said (Mishlei 16:5), "The proud of heart are the abomination of Hashem." One who wishes to acquire the trait of Cleanliness must cleanse himself of all forms of pride and he must know and understand that pride is blindness itself and that man's reason cannot see its defects and recognize its meanness, for if a man could see and recognize the truth, he would depart from all of these evil, destructive elements and remove himself very far from them. We shall speak further of this with the help of Heaven, when we come to the trait of Humility, which, because of the difficulty of its attainment was placed among the last of the traits in the order formulated by R. Pinchas.

We shall now discuss anger. There is the furious man, about whom it was said (Shabbath 105b), "If one becomes angry, it is as if he serves idols." He is angered by any opposition to his will and becomes so filled with wrath that his heart is no longer with him and his judgment vanishes. A man such as he would destroy the entire world if it were within his power to do so, for he is not in any way directed by reason and is as devoid of sensibility as any predatory beast. About him it was said (Job 18:4), "You who tear your soul in your wrath, shall the earth become desolate because of you T' He can easily comrhit any conceivable sin to which his rage brings him, for he is bound by nothing but his anger and he will go where it leads him.

There is another type, who is far removed from the first in degree of anger. He will not become enraged over every lack of conformity with his will, small or great. But when he reaches the point of anger, he will become greatly enraged and give vent to his wrath. It is he whom Chazal characterized (Avos 5.11) as "difficult to arouse and difficult to appease." This form of anger, too, is unquestionably evil, for much that is very damaging may proceed from him during his fit of anger and he will not afterwards be able to straighten what he has made crooked.

There is a lesser form of anger in which one is not easily aroused; and even when he is aroused, his anger is restrained and does not cause him to abandon his intelligence, but he still nurses his wrath. One who becomes angry in this manner stands to lose far less than the others, but there is no question that he has not attained to Cleanliness. What is more, he has not even acquired Watchfulness, for as long as anger moves him, he has not removed himself from the classification of "a man of anger."

There is another who is even less inclined to anger than the aforementioned type. It is very difficult to arouse him, and his anger is neither destructive nor all-consuming, but mild. It lasts no more than a minute, the amount of time it takes from the awakening of anger within him until the awakening of his understanding against it. Chazal characterized him (Ibid.) as "difficult to arouse and easy to appease." His is certainly a goodly portion, for a person's nature moves him to anger and if he masters his anger to the extent that it does not flare strongly and overpower him even during the period of its presence and so that even the small amount of anger that he feels does not linger with him, but passes and departs, he is certainly deserving of praise. Our Sages have said (Chullin 89a), "'He suspends the earth on nothingness' (Job 26:7) - the world endures only because of him who bridles his mouth during a quarrel." The reference is to a situation in which a person has already been awakened to anger, but, mastering his nature, bridles his mouth.

The attribute of Hillel the Elder, however, transcends all of the others, for he took offense at nothing and felt not even a stirring of anger. Such a man is absolutely Clean of anger. Chazal warned against anger even for the sake of a mitzvah, even in a teacher's relationship with his student and in a father's with his son. This is not to say that the offenders should not be reprimanded - they certainly should be; but without anger, with no other purpose than their being set on the right path. Any anger shown to them should be anger of the face and not anger of the heart. Solomon said (Ecclesiastes 7:9), "Do not be hasty-spirited to become angry." And it is stated (Job 5:2), "For the fool is killed by anger." And Chazal said (Eruvin 65b), "A man is recognized in three ways - through his goblet, through his pocket and through his anger."

Envy, too, is nothing but want of reason and foolishness, for the one who envies gains nothing for himself and deprives the one he envies of nothing. He only loses thereby, as is indicated in the verse that I mentioned (Job 5:2), "Envy kills the fool." There are those who are so foolish that if they perceive their neighbor to possess a certain good, they brood and worry and suffer to the point that their neighbor's good prevents them from enjoying their own. As the Sage said (Mishlei 14:30), "Envy is the decay of the bones." There are others who, though not caused much suffering and pain by envy, still experience some hurt. They will at least feel some sinking of spirit upon seeing one rise to a higher level if he is not one of their dearest and closest friends, more so if he is not especially loved by them, and even more so if he is a stranger from a different land. They might say things which would seem to reflect their happiness and thankfulness over his good fortune, but their hearts will be faint within them. This is a very common reaction with most people, for though they may not be characterized by envy, they are still not entirely Clean of it. They are especially affected if one who plies the same trade as they prospers in it for "Every craftsman hates his fellow" (Bereshith Rabbah 19.6), especially if the latter is more successful than he. They will not acknow. ledge and understand the fact that "A man cannot touch even a hair's-breadth of what is set aside for his neighbor" (Yoma 386). If they recognized that everything proceeds from Hashem in accordance with His wondrous judgment and unfathomable wisdom, they would have no reason whatso. ever to suffer over their neighbor's good. This is what the Prophet foretells about the time to come, that Hashem will eradicate this ugly trait from our hearts so that Israel's good will be complete. At that time no one will feel pain over another's good and he who is successful will not be compelled to conceal himself and what relates to him for fear of being envied. As it is written (Isaiah 11:13), "And the envy of Ephraim will depart and the oppressors of Judah will be cut off. Ephraim will not envy Judah ..." This is the kind of peace and serenity experienced by the ministering angels, who all rejoice in their service, each in his place, none envying the other; for seeing the truth to its very depths, they rejoice over the good that they possess and are happy in their portions.

The sister of envy is desire and lust, which wearies a man's heart until the day of his death, as stated by Chazal (Koheleth Rabbah 1.34), "A man does not die with half of his desire fulfilled." There are two main branches of desire, desire for wealth and desire for honor, each as evil as the other and each bringing about many evil consequences.

It is the desire for wealth which binds a man with worldly bonds and places the thongs of labor and preoccupation upon his arms, as it is written (Ecclesiastes 5:9), "The lover of silver will not be satiated with silver." It is this desire which removes one from Divine service, for many prayers are lost and many mitzvos forgotten because of excessive preoccupation and the pursuit of a wealth of stores. This is especially true in relation to Torah study, concerning which Chazal have said (Eruvin 55a), " `It is not across the seas' (Dvarim 30:13) - it does not reside with those who cross the seas for business," and (Avos 2.5), "Not all who engage in business become wise."

The quest for wealth exposes one to many dangers and weakens him with much worrying even after he has acquired a great deal. We also learned (Ibid.), "He who multiplies belongings multiplies worries." And it is this quest which often causes one to trespass against the laws of the Torah and even against the natural laws of reason.

The desire for honor is even greater than the desire for wealth, for it is possible for a person to overcome his inclination for wealth and the other pleasures and still be pressed by the desire for honor, being unable to tolerate being, and seeing himself beneath his friends.

Many were caught and destroyed by the desire for honor. Jeroboam ben Nevat was barred from the World to Come only as a result of his desire for honor. As was stated by Chazal (Sanhedrin 102a), "Hashem seized his garment and said to him, `Repent, and you and I and the son of Jesse will promenade in the Garden of Eden.' Jeroboam asked, `Who will go first?' Hashem answered, `The son of Jesse:' and Jeroboam said, `If so, I refuse.' " What, if not the desire for honor, brought about the destruction of Korach and his entire congregation? As Scripture explicitly states (Numbers 16:10), "And would you also seek the priesthood? " Chazal have told us (Bamidbar Rabbah 18.1) that his entire rebellion stemmed from his seeing Elizaphan ben Uziel as prince and desiring to be prince in his place. This same desire, according to Chazal (Zohar to Numbers 13:3), was responsible for the spies' speaking ill of the land, thus bringing about their death and the death of the entire generation. They feared a diminution of their honor in the possibility that after entry into the land they would no longer be princes of Israel and others would be appointed in their place. What, if not a concern for his honor caused Saul to begin to seek an opportunity to kill David? As it is written (1 Samuel 18:7ff), "And the exultant wopeople answered and said, 'Saul has slain ...' and Saul eyed David from that day forward." What, if not concern for his honor, caused Joab to kill Amasa? (For David had said to Amasa (11 Samuel 19:14), "... if you will not always be my general...")

In fine, the desire for honor tugs at a person's heart more than any of the other longings and desires in the world. If not for concern over his honor, a person would be content to eat whatever was at hand, to clothe himself with whatever would cover his nakedness, and to dwell in a house which would afford him protection from the elements. He would obtain his livelihood with little effort and would feel no need to exert himself to become rich. But so as not to see himself as lower and lesser than his friends, he places a yoke upon his neck, and there is no end to all his labors. It is with this in mind that our Teachers of blessed memory said (Avos 4.20), "Envy, lust and honor-seeking remove a person from the world," and warned us (Ibid. 6.4), "Do not seek greatness or desire honor." How many starve themselves and stoop to feeding themselves from charity so as not to engage in an occupation which they feel is lacking in respectability, for fear of a diminution of their honor? Is there anything sillier? They prefer to dwell in idleness, which leads to stagnation, lewdness and theft, and to all of the major sins in order not to lower themselves and detract from the honor which they imagine themselves to possess. Chazal, who constantly exhorted us to follow the path of truth and conducted us upon it, said (Avos 1.9), "Love work and hate position," and (Pesachim 113a), "Flay a carcass in the marketplace and do not say, `I am an important person; I am a priest,' " and (Bava Bathra 110a), "A man should rather do work that is strange to him than have need of others."

In fine, the desire for honor is one of man's greatest stumbling blocks. He cannot be a faithful servant to his Master as long as he is concerned with his own honor; for whatever the case, his foolishness will lead him to detract from the honor of Heaven. As King David, may Peace be upon him, said (II Samuel 6:22), "I will become even lesser than this; I will become low in my eyes." The only true honor is true knowledge of the Torah. In the words of Chazal (Avos 6.3), "There is no honor but Torah, as it is said (Mishlei 3:35), `The wise will inherit honor.' " Anything else is seeming, delusive honor, completely meaningless and worthless. One who would be Clean should cleanse himself of the desire for honor and purify himself of it; he will then be successful.

I have discussed up to this point many particulars of Cleanliness. What has been said should serve as a model for all of the other mitzvos and traits. "The wise man man will hear and add to his wisdom and the man of understanding will acquire stratagems " (Mishlei 1:5).

I cannot deny that the acquisition of Cleanliness requires a little effort, but I still keep that it does not entail so much effort as appearances would lead one to believe. It is more difficult in the thinking than in the doing. If one takes it into his heart and resolutely determines to be among the possessors of this good trait, then, with a little habituation, he will easily acquire it - far more easily than he could have imagined. This is borne out by experience.

CHAPTER XII

CONCERNING THE MEANS OF ACQUIRING CLEANLINESS

THE TRUE MEANS of acquiring Cleanliness is perpetual study of both the halachic and ethical pronouncements of Chazal. For once the truth of man's responsibility for Cleanliness and his need for it has impressed itself upon a person through his prior acquisition of Watchfulness and Zeal, (the result of his occupation with the means toward their attainment and the withdrawing of himself from the elements detracting from them) - once this truth has impressed itself upon a person, he will, with a knowledge of the fine points of the mitzvos, be enabled to exercise Watchfulness in relation to all of them, so that no deterrents will prevent his attaining to Cleanliness.

Of necessity, one must acquire a thorough knowledge of the laws, which will enable him to determine how far the mitzvos branch out. Also, because one is prone to forgetfulness in relation to these fine distinctions, he must always engage in the study of those treatises which expound them, so that the distinctions are enforced within his mind. 1n doing so, he will, of a certainty, be spurred on to observe them.

Likewise, the cultivation of character traits demands a study of the ethical dicta of the earlier or later authorities. For very often, even after one has resolved to be fastidious in Cleanliness, he is liable to wrongdoing in certain areas because of their not having come within the province of his understanding. For a man is not born wise, and it is impossible for him to know everything. But in studying these writings he will be awakened to that which he had not recognized, and he will come to understand what he had not previously grasped, even such matters as he will not find in the treatises themselves. For when his mind is alive to these things, it will survey all within its domain and bring forth new understandings from the wellspring of truth.

The factors which detract from Cleanliness are all those which detract from Watchfulness, in addition to that of incomprehensive knowledge of the laws or of ethical principles, as stated above. As Chazal have said (Avos 2.5), "An ignoramus cannot be a saint" (for he who does not know, cannot do), and, in a similar vein (Kiddushin 406), "Great is learning, for it leads to doing."

CHAPTER XIII

CONCERNING THE TRAIT OF SEPARATION

SEPARATION IS THE BEGINNING of Saintliness. Up to this point we have concerned ourselves with the requirements for righteousness. From this point on we shall discuss the requirements for Saintliness. It is to be observed that Separation bears the same relationship to Saintliness as Watchfulness does to Zeal, the first element in each set concerning itself with departing from evil and the second with doing good. The rationale of Separation is epitomized in the words of Chazal (Yevamoth 20a), "Sanctify yourself through what is permitted to you." This is the signification of the word "separation" itself i.e. separating and withdrawing oneself from something, forbidding to oneself something which is permitted. The intent is to keep oneself from that which is forbidden, the understanding being that a person should withdraw and separate himself from anything which might give rise to something that could bring about evil, even though it does not bring it about at the moment and even though it is not evil in itself.

If you look into the matter you will perceive three distinct levels - the forbidden things themselves, their fences (the edicts and safeguards that Chazal made binding on all of Israel), and the "withdrawals" that those committed to Separation must create for themselves by circumscribing themselves and building fences for themselves; that is, by abstaining from things which were permitted, which were not proscribed to all of Israel, and separating themselves from them so as to be far removed from evil.

One might ask, "What basis is there for multiplying prohibitions? Have Chazal not said (Yerushalmi Nedarim 9.1), `Are the Torah's prohibitions not enough for you that you come to create new prohibitions for yourself?' Have Chazal in their great wisdom not seen what it was necessary to forbid as a safeguard; and have they not already forbidden it? And does it not follow, then, that anything which they did not proscribe they felt should be permitted? Then why should we now initiate edicts which they felt no need for? What is more, there is no limiting anything like this. One would have to live in desolation and affliction, deriving no enjoyment whatever from the world, whereas Chazal have said (Yerushalmi Kiddushin 4:12) that a man will have to give an accounting to the Presence for everything that his eyes beheld and he did not wish to eat, though permitted and able to do so. They adduced Scripture in their support (Ecclesiastes 2:10), `Anything my eyes asked, I did not keep from them.' "

The answer to these arguments is that Separation is certainly necessary and essential. Chazal exhorted us concerning it (Sifra)," `Be holy' (Leviticus 19:2)separate yourselves," and (Ta'anith I la), "One who engages in fasting is called "holy," a fact which may be deduced from the case of a Nazarite;" and (Pesikta) " `The righteous man eats to the contentment of his soul' (Mishlei 13:25) - this is Hezekiah, King of Judah, about whom it is said that two bunches of vegetables and one litra of meat were brought before him each day, while the Jews made mock, saying, `This is a King?' " In relation to Rabbeinu Hakadosh they said (Kethuvoth 104a) that before he died he held up his ten fingers and said, "It is perfectly known to You that I derived no enjoyment from this world, not even to the extent of my little finger." And along the same lines they said (Yalkut Devarim 830), "Before a man prays that words of Torah be absorbed into his innards, let him pray that food and drink not be absorbed therein."

All of these statements explicitly point out one's need and responsibility for Separation. In any event, we must account for the statements to the contrary. The truth is that many distinctions and principles must be considered. There is a type of Separation which we are duty-bound to observe and a type that we were warned not to fall victim to -- in the words of King Solomon, may Peace be upon him (Ecclesiustes 7:16), "Do not be over-righteous."

We shall now discuss the desirable type of Separation. Having recognized the fact that all of the world's contingencies are trials to a man, as stated and verified above, and having been made convincingly aware of man's weakness and the nearness of his mind to evil, we must perforce conclude that a man should attempt to escape these contingencies as far as possible so as better to protect himself from the evil upon which they border. For there is no wordly pleasure upon whose heels some sin does not follow. For example, food and drink when free of all dietary prohibitions are permitted, but filling oneself brings in its wake the putting off of the yoke of Heaven, and drinking of wine brings in its wake licentiousness and other varieties of evil. This obtains to an even greater degree if one accustoms himself to eating and drinking to satiety. If he is once made to lack his usual fare he will be painfully aware of the fact and will thrust himself into the -hegt of the race for possessions and property so that his table will be spread in accordance with his desires. He will thence be drawn on to wrongdoing and theft, and thence to taking oaths and to all of the other sins that follow in its wake; and he will depart from Divine service, from Torah and from prayer, all of which would not have occurred if, from the beginning, he had not allowed himself to be pulled into these pleasures. As Chazal have said in relation to the rebellious son (Sanhedrin 72a), "The Torah penetrates to the very end of a person's thoughts

..." And in relation to licentiousness they said (Sotah 2a), "One who sees a Sotah in her disgrace should forbid wine to himself." You will notice that this is an excellent device for the rescuing of oneself from his evil inclination; for since it is difficult for one to conquer and subdue it when he is involved in the transgression, he must, while he is far from it, remove himself yet farther so that it will be difficult for his evil inclination to bring him close to the transgression.

There is no question as to the permissibility of cohabitation with one's wife, but still, ablutions were instituted for those who had had seminal emissions, so that Scholars should not be steadily with their wives, like roosters. Even though the act itself is permissible it implants in a person a lust for it which might draw him on to what is forbidden; as Chazal have said (Sukkah 526), "There is a small organ in a man which, when it is satiated, hungers and which, when it is made to hunger, is sated." And they said about R. Eleazar (Nedarim 20b) that even in the proper hour and the correct time he would expose a handbreadth and conceal two hand-breadths and imagine that a demon was compelling him, in order to cancel out the feeling of pleasure.

The Torah did not exhort us in relation to the beauty and style of clothing and adornments, requiring for their permissibility only that they not contain a mixture of wool and linen and that they be fitted with tzitzith. But who is not aware of the fact that fancy headgear and embroidered material pulls one toward pride and brings one to the border of licentiousness, aside from giving rise to envy, lust and exploitation, which attach to anything that is very desirable to a person. And Chazal have already remarked (Bereshith Rabbah 22.6), "As soon as the evil inclination sees a man assuming delicate stances, straightening his garments and curling his hair, it says, 'He is mine.' "

Walking and talking which do not involve any particular prohibition are certainly permissible, but how much neglect of Torah grows out of it, how much slander, how many lies, how much levity; as it is said (Mishlei 10:19), "In a multitude of words there is no ceasing of sin."

In fine, since all the world's contingencies are great dangers, how commendable is the attitude of him who desires to escape them and of him who increases his distance from them. His Separation is the desirable type, the type in which a person takes from the world, in all of the uses that he makes of it, only what his nature renders absolutely essential to him. It was this type of Separation which R. Judah reveled in when he said (in a statement previously referred to) that he had derived no enjoyment from this world, not even to the extent of his little finger, though he was a Prince of Israel and his table was a table of kings, entirely commensurate with the dignity of his station. As Chazal said (Avodah Zarah 1 la), "'There are two nations in your womb' (Bereishis 25:23) - this refers to R. Judah and Antoninus, from whose table were never lacking lettuce, cucumbers and radishes, neither in the dry nor in the rainy seasons." This was the case, too, with Hezekiah, King of Judah. And all of the other statements to which I have referred stress the importance of a person's separating himself from all worldly pleasures so as not to fall into the dangers connected with them.

It may occur to you to ask, "Why, if Separation is so necessary and essential, did our Sages not institute it as they did the `fences' and other measures?" The answer is clear and simple. "Our Sages pronounced an edict only if the majority of the people could abide by it" (Bava Kamma 79b); and the majority of the people cannot be saintly. It is enough if they are righteous. But upon the select few who desire to achieve closeness to Hashem and to benefit thereby all those who depend upon them, devolves the fulfillment of the Tzaddikim' higher duties, those duties which the others cannot fulfill, namely, the provisions of Separation here set forth. This is the will of Hashem; for since it is impossible for all of the individuals within a nation to be on an identical level (levels varying in accordance with intelligence), those individuals who have not completely conditioned themselves for the reception of the love of Hashem and of His Divine Presence are enabled to attain to it through the chosen few who have. As Chazal said in relation to the four species of the lulav (Vayikra Rabbah 30.11), "Let these come and atone for these,." And we find in relation to the incident of Ulah bar Koshev (Yerushalmi Terumoth 8.4) that when R. Joshua ben Levi asked Elijah of blessed memory, "Is it not a Mishnah ?" the latter replied, "But is it a Mishnah for Tzaddikim?"

The undesirable type of separation is that of the foolish gentiles who abstain not only from that which is not essential to them, but also from that which is, punishing their bodies with strange forms of affliction that Hashem has no desire for. What is more, our Sages have said (Ta'anith 226), "A person is forbidden to torture himself." And in relation to charity they said (Yerushalmi, conclusion of Peah), "Anyone who needs it and does not take it, is a spiller of blood;" and (Ta'anith 22b), " `A living soul' (Bereishis 2:7) -sustain the soul that I gave to you;" and (Ta'anith I 1 a), "One who engages in fasting is called `a sinner.' " (This they applied to a person who is in no condition to fast.) And Hillel was wont to apply (Mishlei 11:17), "He who is kind to his soul is a man of saintliness," to the eating of the morning meal. He made it a practice to wash his face and hands for the honor of his Master, reasoning from the practice that prevailed at that time of washing the statues of the kings (Vayikra Rabbah 34.3).

The truth, then, is that a man should separate himself from anything which is not essential to him in relation to the affairs of the world; if he separates himself from anything which is essential to him, regardless of the reason for its being so, he is a sinner. This principle is a consistent on.-. Its application to particular instances, however, is a matter of individual judgment (and "A man will be praised according to his understanding"). For it is impossible to discuss all the particulars of Separation; they are so numerous that the mind cannot encompass them. One must deal with them each in its own time.

CHAPTER XIV

CONCERNING THE DIVISIONS OF SEPARATION

THERE ARE THREE parts to Separation: pleasures, laws, and conduct respectively.

Separation in relation to pleasures, which we spoke of in the previous chapter, consists in one's taking from the world only what is essential to him. This type of Separation encompasses anything which provides pleasure to any one of the senses, whether the pleasure be gained through food, cohabitation, clothing, strolls, conversation or similar means, exceptions obtaining only at such times when deriving pleasure through these means is a mitzvah.

Separation in the law is being stringent to the extent of taking cognizance of even a sole dissenting view in a controversy if there is justice to it, even if the law is not decided in accordance with it, and in not taking the easier alternative in cases of doubt, though permitted to do so. Chazal explained (Chullin 376) the statement of Ezekiel (4:14), "My soul was not polluted" - "I did not eat of an animal about which a sage had to make a decision," and, "I did not eat the flesh of an animal that had to be slaughtered quickly." Though permitted by law to eat of these animals, he was stringent with himself and did not.

It has already been indicated that those who practice Separation may not guide themselves by what is permitted to all of Israel, but must withdraw themselves from what is repulsive, from what is similar to it, and from what is similar to what is similar to it. As Mar Ukvah said (Chullin 105a), "I am to my father as vinegar derived from wine; for my father, if he would eat meat today, would not eat cheese until tomorrow at the same time, whereas I, though I would not eat cheese at the next meal, would do so the meal following that." Now there is no question that the practice of Mar Ukvah's father does not constitute the law in the matter, for if it did, Mar Ukvah would certainly never have gone against it. It is just that his father was stringent in his Separation. And it is because Mar Ukvah was not on a par with his father in this trait that he compared himself to vinegar and his father to wine.

Separation in relation to conduct is secluding and separating himself from society in order to turn to Divine service and to proper reflection upon it. In this one must be careful to avoid extremes; for Chazal have stated (Kesuvos 17a), "A man's mind should always be associated with his fellow men," and (Ta'anith 7a), " `A sword upon those who scheme and are undone' (Jeremiah 50:36) - a sword upon the enemies of Scholars who isolate themselves and occupy themselves with Torah." The proper course to follow is to associate with reputable persons for as long necessary in the interest of Torah study or of earning a livelihood and then to seclude oneself for the purpose of communing with Hashem and attaining to ways of righteousness and to true Divine service. Included in this type of Separation is limiting one's conversation, being careful not to engage in idle talk, not gazing outside of one's four ells, and all other restrictions governing similar activities which might become second nature if they were not so restricted.

It may be seen that though these three divisions have been treated in the form of short principles, they take in many of man's activities. And I have already indicated that it is impossible to set forth all of the particulars, but that they must be derived by individual judgment through reference to the principles and the truths underlying them.

CHAPTER XV

CONCERNING THE MEANS OF ACQUIRING SEPARATION

THE BEST WAY for a man to acquire Separation is to regard the inferior quality of the pleasures of this world, both in point of their ova n insignificance and in point of the great evils to which they are prone to give rise. For what inclines one's nature to these pleasures to the extent that he requires so much strength and scheming to separate himself from them is the gullibility of the eyes, their tendency to be deceived by good and pleasing superficial appearances. It was this deception which led to the commission of the first sin. As Scripture testifies (Bereishis 3:6), "And the woman saw that the tree was good to eat from and that it was desirable to the eyes ... and she took of its fruit and ate." But when it becomes clear to a person that this "good" is deceptive and illusive, that it has no healthy permanence, and that it contains real evil oi is prone to give rise to it, he will certainly come to despise and decline it. All that a man need teach his intelligence, then, is to recognize the weakness and falseness of these pleasures so that he will naturally come to despise them and find it not at all difficult to spurn them.

There is no pleasure more basic and more pronounced than that of eating. Yet is there anything more evanescent? The food that is enjoyed is the size of a person's throat, and once it leaves the throat to descend into the intestines, its memory is lost and the food is forgotten, as if it had never existed.

Enough black bread will satiate one to the same extent as fattened swans.

One will be made especially aware of the truth of what is being said if he considers the many sicknesses connected with eating or at least the heaviness that one experiences after meals and the vapors that becloud [variant: confound] his brain. These considerations would unquestionably cause one to spurn the pleasure of eating, showing its good to be not truly good and its evil to be truly evil. Similarly, an analysis of all of the other worldly pleasures would reveal that even their illusory good endures only a short time and that the evil which can grow out of them is so severe and prolonged, that no reasoning individual would consent to expose himself to the evil dangers that they present for the sake of the small amount of good which they offer. This is self-evident. If one accustoms himself to constant reflection upon this truth, he will extricate himself little by little from the bonds of ignorance with which the darkness of earthiness binds him, and he will no longer be deceived by illusory pleasures. He will then come to despise them and to realize that he should take from the world only that which is essential to him, as I have written above. But just as thinking upon this truth leads to the acquisition of the trait of Separation, so does ignoring it hinder such acquisition, as does courting the company of those who pursue honor and multiply vanity. For when one regards their elegance and dignity, it is impossible that his lust will not be awakened to desire these things. And even if he will not permit his evil inclination to conquer him, he will, in any event, not escape the battle and its dangers. This is the intent of Solomon's statement (Ecclesiastes 7:2), "It is better to go to the house of mourning than to the house of feasting."

More desirable than anything else, however, in respect to the attainment of Separation, is solitude; for when one removes worldly goods from before his eyes, he removes desire for them from his heart. As David said in praise of solitude (Tehillim 55:7), "Who will give me the wings of a dove ... I would wander far off; I would lie down in the desert." We find that the Prophets Elijah and Elisha situated themselves in the mountains in keeping with their practice of seclusion; and the Sages, the first Tzaddikim, of blessed memory followed in their footsteps, for they found this practice the most effective means of acquiring perfection in Separation and protecting themselves from being led into vanities by those of their neighbors.

What one must be heedful of in the process of acquiring Separation is not to desire to leap to its farthest reaches in one moment, for he will certainly not be able to make such great strides. He should rather proceed in Separation, little by little, acquiring a little today and adding a little more tomorrow, until he is so habituated to it that it is second nature with him.

CHAPTER XVI

CONCERNING THE TRAIT OF PURITY

PURITY REFERS to the perfection of one's heart and thoughts, as indicated in David's statement (Tehillim 51:12), "Create in me, Hashem, a pure heart." The intent of this trait is that a man leave no room in his deeds for the evil inclination, but conduct himself in accordance with intelligence and fear of G -d, uninfluenced by sin and lust. This applies even to physical, earthy actions; for even after one has accustomed himself to Separation so that he takes from the world only what is essential, he must still purify his heart and thoughts so that, even in taking the little that he does, he is motivated not by desire for enjoyment and lust, but by thought for the good which proceeds from his actions in respect to wisdom and Divine service, as was said of R. Eliezer (Nedarim 20b), "He would expose one hand-breadth and conceal two handbreadths and imagine that he was being compelled by a demon." He derived no pleasure whatosever, but performed the act only with a thought to the mitzvah and Divine service. Along these lines Solomon said (Mishlei 3:6), "In all your ways know Him and He will straighten your paths."

It must be borne in mind, however, that just as the concept of purity of thought is applicable to bodily deeds - which by their nature border on the realm of the evil inclination - in the sense of one's withdrawing them from it so that they do not come to appertain to it, so is this concept applicable to worthy deeds, close to the realm of the Creator, may His Name be blessed, in the sense of one's not setting them far from Him and not permitting them to enter the province of the evil inclination. This is what underlies the idea of "not for the sake of the mitzvah itself" which is often mentioned by our Teachers of blessed memory. However, it is clear from their words that there are various kinds of "not for the sake of the mitzvah itself," the worst being the type in which one serves not for the purpose of Divine service at all, but in order to deceive people or to gain honor or wealth. About such a one it is said (Yerushalmi Berachoth 1.2), "It were better had he been smothered in his placenta." And the Prophet says about him (Isaiah 64:5), "We have all become as one unclean, and all our righteousness as a soiled garment." Ano,.,er type of "not for the sake of the mitzvah itself" is serving for the sake of reward, about which it is said (Pesachim 506), "A person should always occupy himself with Torah and mitzvos, even if not for the sake of the mitzvah itself, for doing so will lead him to serve for the the sake of the mitzvah itself." There is no question, though, that one who has not yet attained to the latter mode of service is far from attaining his perfection.

That, however, in relation to which one requires greater insight and effort is the intrusion of a forbidden element into his motives. For sometimes one embarks upon a mitzvah entirely for its own sake, our Father in Heaven having decreed it, but does not prevent himself thereby from incorporating some other motive such as desire for praise or reward into his deed. And sometimes, though he may not desire to be praised, still, in rejoicing over the praise that he receives, he might come to take greater pains than he normally would, as in the case of R. Chanina ben Teradyon's daughter (Avodah Zarah 18a), who overhearing some people remark about her graceful stride, "How beautifully that girl walks," immediately sought, because of this praise, to display even more grace.

Though an undesirable motive may be outweighed by the major intention behind a deed, still, the deed which contains such a motive is not completely pure. And just as it is not permissible to offer up upon the earthly altar any but the cleanest flour, sifted through thirteen sieves (Menachoth 76b) and therefore entirely free of any impurity, so is it impossible to offer up upon the Heavenly altar so that they will be accepted as representing perfect, choice, Divine service, any but the choicest of actions, entirely free of imperfections. I am not suggesting that anything which does not come up to this standard will be completely rejected, for Hashem does not withhold the reward of any creature, but rewards good deeds in accordance with their worth. What I am saying is that perfect Divine service, the type which should be characteristic of all those who love Hashem in truth, is that which is entirely pure, that which is directed to Hashem only and to nothing else besides. Anything which falls short of this standard, to the extent that it falls short, is lacking in perfection. As King David, may Peace be upon him, said (Tehillim 73:25), "Who is mine in Heaven and I want none beside You on earth" and, in the same vein (Ibid. 119:140), "Your word is very pure and Your servant loves it."

The fact is that true Divine service must be far purer than gold and silver, as David says about Torah (Ibid. 12:7), "The words of Hashem are pure words, silver purified in a crucible upon the earth, refined seven times." One who serves Hashem in truth will not content himself with little in this respect and will not consent to take silver mixed with dross and lead, that is, Divine service mixed with impure motives. He will insist upon that which is suitably clean and pure, and will then be called "the performer of a mitzvah as it is explicitly stated," about which Chazal say (Shabbath 63a), "One who performs a mitzvah as it is explicitly stated receives no evil tidings."

And, similarly (Nedarim 62a), "Do things for the sake of their Creator and speak about them for their own sake." It is this type of service that is chosen by those who serve Hashem with a whole heart. For one who does not cleave to Hashem with true love will find such purification extremely tedious and burdensome. He will say, "Who can endure it? We are earthy creatures, born of woman. We can never expect to attain to such great purity." Those, however, who love Hashem and desire to serve Him will rejoice in showing the steadfastness of their love for Hashem and in strengthening themselves in refining and purifying it. This is the intent of David's conclusion, "And your servant loves it." And in truth, this is the criterion by which the lovers of Hashem are judged and evaluated. For one who is more skillful in purifying his heart is closer to Hashem and more beloved by Him. It was such purity that characterized "the first ones in the land" who strengthened themselves and were victorious, our forefathers and the other shepherds who purified their hearts before Him. As David forewarned Solomon his son (I Chronicles 28:9), "For Hashem searches all hearts and understands the inclination of all thoughts," and as Chazal have said (Sanhedrin 1066), "The Merciful One desires the heart." For it is not enough to the Master, Blessed be He, if one's deeds are deeds of mitzvah. What is of paramount importance to Him is that one's heart be pure for dedication to true Divine service. The heart is the king and mover of all the parts of the body. If it does not bring itself to serve Hashem, then the service of the other organs is meaningless, for they function as the heart directs them. And as Scripture explicitly states (Mishlei 23:26), "Give your heart to me my son."

CHAPTER XVII

CONCERNING THE MEANS OF ACQUIRING PURITY

ONE WHO HAS ALREADY persevered and acquired the aforementioned traits will find it easy to acquire the trait of Purity, for when he will consider and contemplate the inferior quality of worldly pleasures and worldly goods, he will come to despise them and to regard them as evils and as defects of earthy, dark, gross nature. When the truth of this understanding impresses itself upon him, there is no question that he will find it easy to separate himself from them and remove them from his heart. The more time one devotes to thinking deeply into the matter in order to recognize the lowly nature of earthiness and of its pleasures, the easier he will find it to purify his thoughts and his heart so that they have no recourse to the evil inclination in any deed whatsoever; and his role in any earthy activities that he does perform will be one of compulsion only.

But just as we have divided purity of thought into two sections, one dealing with bodily actions and the other with Divine service, so are there two distinct operations required for their acquisition. To purify one's thoughts in relation to one's bodily actions, a person must engage in constant observation of the inferior nature of the world and of its pleasures, as stated above. And to purify his thoughts in relation to Divine service, he must give much thought to the falseness of pride and its deceits, and train himself to flee from pride. If he does so, he will be clean during the time of his Divine service of any strivings for the praises and encomiums of men, and his mind will be directed solely to our Lord, who is our praise, and all our good, and our perfection, and beside whom there is nothing, as it is said (Dvarim 10:21), "He is your praise and He is your Hashem."

One of the means which lead a person to the acquisition of this trait is preparation for Divine service and mitzvos, by virtue of which he does not enter into the performance of a mitzvah suddenly, lacking the presence of mind to think about what he is doing, but instead readies himself for it and slowly prepares his heart for thought. He will then consider what he is going to do and before Whom he is going to do it, and so considering, it will be easy for him to divest himself of any exterior motives and to implant in his heart motives which are true and desirable. The early Tzaddikim would wait one hour before they prayed so that their hearts would be directed to the Presence (Berachoth 30b). It goes without saying that they did not allow their hearts to remain idle for an hour, but deliberated and readied them for the prayer that was to follow by casting foreign thoughts from themselves and filling their hearts with the requisite love and fear. In the words of Job (Job 11:13), "If you have prepared your heart, spread out your hands to Him."

The deterrents to this trait, those elements which constitute a lack of attention to the aforementioned factors, are ignorance of the inferior quality of worldly pleasures, pursuit of honor, and insufficient preparation for Divine service. The first two seduce the mind and pull it toward exterior motives, so that it becomes like an adulteress, who, while still living with her husband, takes in strangers. Foreign thoughts are referred to as the adultery of the heart, as it is written (Numbers 15:39), "And do not turn aside after your hearts and after your eyes, which you follow adulterously." In entertaining foreign thoughts, the heart turns from the honest outlook with which it should become identified to vanities and deceitful appearances.

Insufficient preparation for Divine service fosters the natural ignorance which proceeds from the indivorceable element of earthiness in man and which befouls Divine service with its stench.

We shall now discuss the trait of Saintliness.

CHAPTER XVIII

CONCERNING THE TRAIT OF SAINTLINESS

THE TRAIT of Saintliness does indeed require much explanation, for many customs and practices pass-among many for Saintliness, which are nothing but the shells of Saintliness, wanting in form, feature, and perfection. This is attributable to a lack of close observation and honest reasoning on the part of the practitioners of this artificial form of saintliness. Instead of exerting and wearying themselves to know the way of Hashem with clear, rational knowledge, they proceed in saintliness on the basis of what upon first thought happens to strike them as being saintly, without submitting their ideas to an examination in depth and weighing them upon the scales of wisdom. It is because of them that Saintliness has become repulsive to most people, the intelligentsia among them. For the pseudo-Tzaddikim give the impression that Saintliness lies in foolishness and runs counter to intelligence and logic; and they lead people to believe that Saintliness consists entirely in the reciting of many supplications, in lengthy confessions, in exaggerated wailings and bowings, and in esoteric flagellations (such as immersion in ice and snow, and the like) by which a person mortifies himself. They do not realize that even though some of these things are required for those engaged in repentance and some are appropriate for those who practice Separation, Saintliness is not founded upon them at all (although the very best of these practices may serve as complements to Saintliness).

The fact is that it requires great depth to correctly grasp the essence of Saintliness, for it rests upon the foundations of higher wisdom and upon a perfection of one's deeds so complete as to serve as a goal for all who are wise at heart. And, indeed, it is only the wise who can truthfully acquire it. As Chazal have said (Avos 2:5), "An ignoramus cannot be a Saint."

We shall now explain the concept of Saintliness in ordered sequence. The root of Saintliness is epitomized in the statement of Chazal (Berachoth 17a), "Fortunate is the man whose toil is in Torah and gives pleasure to his Creator." The underlying idea is this: It is known which mitzvos are binding on all of Israel and to what extent one is bound by them. However, one who truly loves the Creator may His Name be blessed, will not endeavor and intend to fulfill his obligations by means of the duty which is acknowledged by all of Israel in general, but will react in very much the same manner as a son who loves his father, who, even if his father gives only a slight indication of desiring something, undertakes to fulfill this desire as completely as he can. And though the father may air his desire only once, and even then, incompletely, it is enough for such a son just to understand the inclination of his father's mind to do for him even what has not been expressly requested. If he can understand by himself what will bring pleasure to his father, he will not wait to be commanded more explicitly or to be told a second time.

We notice at all periods and at all times, between all lovers and friends - between a man and his wife, between a father and his son, in fine, between all those who are bound with a love which is truly strong -that the lover will not say, "I have not been commanded further. What I have been told to do explicitly is enough for me." He will rather attempt, by analyzing the commands, to arrive at the intention of the commander and to do what he judges will give him pleasure. The same holds true for one who strongly loves his Creator; for he, too, is one of the class of lovers. The mitzvos, whose behests are clear and widely known, will serve as an indication to him of the will and desire of Hashem. He will not say, "What has been explicitly stated is enough for me," or "In any event I will discharge my obligations by doing what is incumbent upon me." To the contrary, he will say, "Since I have seen that G- d's desire inclines toward this, I will use it as a sign to do as much as I can in relation to it and to extend it into as many areas as I can envisage Hashem's desiring its being extended into." Such a man may be called "one who gives pleasure to his Creator."

Saintliness, then, is a comprehensive performance of all the mitzvos, embracing all of the relevant areas and conditions within the realm of possibility. It is to be seen that Saintliness is of the same nature as Separation, differing from it only in the respect that it concerns the positive commandments whereas Separation deals with the negative ones, but corresponding to it in terms of general function, which is adding to what has been explicitly stated that which we may deduce from the explicit commandment as giving pleasure to Hashem. This is the delimitation of true Saintliness. I shall now explain its chief divisions.

CHAPTER XIX

CONCERNING THE DIVISIONS OF SAINTLINESS

THERE ARE three principal divisions of Saintliness, one involving the deed; the second, the manner of performance; and the third, the intention. The division of deed is itself divided into two areas, one concerning the relationship between man and the Presence, and the second, that between man and his neighbor.

Saintliness of deed in the relationship between man and the Presence consists in the performance of the mitzvos with all their fine points as far as is physically possible. Chazal referred to these fine points as "the remnants of a mitzvah" and said (Sukkah 38a), "The remnants of a Mitzvah ward off accidents." The fact that the body of a mitzvah may be fulfilled without these "remnants" and one's obligation discharged thereby, is a consideration for the overall body of Jews, but those who would be Saintly must increase their fulfillment of them and certainly not decrease it.

Saintliness of deed in the relationship between man and his neighbor consists in the doing of good in abundance, in one's always benefiting his fellow creatures and never injuring them. This applies to the body, belongings and soul of one's neighbor.

Body : One must seek to help all people in any way he can, and lighten their burdens. As we learned (Avos 6.6), "And bearing a burden with one's neighbor." If he can prevent some bodily harm from coming to his neighbor or remove that which threatens such harm, he must exert himself to do so.

Belongings : One must assist his neighbor as far as his resources allow and guard his belongings against damage in every way he can. He must especially take precautions to see to it that he himself is in no way responsible for causing such damage, whether to single individuals or to many. And though there may be no immediate cause for concern, still if there is even a possibility that anything belonging to him will cause damage, he must get it out of the way. Chazal have said (Avos 2.12), "Your neighbor's belongings should be as precious to you as your own."

Soul : One must strive to give his neighbor as much pleasure as he can, whether in respect to honor or to anything else. Anything which he can do which he knows will give his neighbor pleasure, is a mitzvah of Saintliness for him to do. It goes without saying that he must not cause his neighbor any pain whatsoever in any manner whatsoever. All of this comes within the framework of lovingkindness, the worth and binding nature of which Chazal were boundless in affirming. Included in this area is the pursuit of peace, the general promotion of good in the relationship between man and his neighbor.

I will now substantiate all of these statements by reference to the words of Chazal, although what I have said is obvious and needs no substantiation. In the chapter Bnei Ha'ir it is said (Megillah 27b ff), "R. Zakkai was asked by his disciples, `Why have you merited such long life?' He answered, `I never urinated within four ells of prayer, I never called my friend by a nickname and I never missed making Kiddush on the Sabbath. I had an old mother. Once she sold her hat and bought me wine for Kiddush.' " This is an instance of Saintliness in relation to the fine points of mitzvos, for since R. Zakkai was so lacking in means that in order to procure wine his mother had to sell her hat, he was not required to obtain wine in the first place. For him to do so, then, was an act of Saintliness. And his being concerned for his friend's honor to the extent that he would not even call him by a completely non-objectionable nickname (according to Tosafoth's interpretation) was also a facet of Saintliness. R. Huna tied elastic upon his garments because he had sold his girdle to buy wine for Kiddush. "R. Eliezer ben Shammuah was asked by his disciples (Ibid.), `Why have you merited such long life?' He answered, `I never used the synagogue as a short-cut and I never walked above the heads of the holy people while they were seated at their studies." In the first instance, R. Huna was practising Saintliness in the honoring of a synagogue; and in the second, by not walking among the seated scholars in order not to give the impression that he was belittling them, he was honoring his fellow creatures. "R. Preida was asked by his disciples, `Why have you merited such long life?' He answered, `No one ever preceded me to the house of study; I never recited the blessing before a Kohen and 1 never ate of an animal whose gift-offerings had not been taken. ' " "R. Nechunia was asked, `Why have you merited such long life?' He answered, `I never derived honor through the shame of my friend, and the curse of my friend never went up upon my bed."' By way of illustration we are told, "R. Huna, when R. Chana bar Chanilai came along and relieved him of an axe that he had been carrying upon his shoulder, said to him, 'If it is customary for you to carry it where you come from, then you may carry it, but if it is not, I have no wish to gain honor through your dishonor."' Even though "the shame of his friend" implies a conscious attempt to increase one's honor through the shaming of one's friend, those who are Saintly are averse to acquiring honor through the dishonor of their friends even if the latter are quite agreeable to their doing so. It was in relation to Saintliness, too, that R. Zeira was speaking when he said, "I was never officious in my own household, I never walked in front of one greater than I, I never meditated in unclean places, I never walked four ells without Torah and Tefillin, I never slept or napped in the synagogue, I never rejoiced in my neighbor's misfortune and I never called my friend by his nickname." Represented here are all the types of Saintliness mentioned above. Chazal state further (Bava Kama 30a), "R. Yehudah said, `If one wishes to be a Saint, let him fulfill the laws of Benedictions' (i.e those laws governing the relationship between man and his Master). Others say, `Let him fulfill the laws of Damages' (i.e. those laws governing the relationship between man and his neighbor). And others say, `Let him fulfill the laws of Ethics' " (which comprise both categories).

The practice of lovingkindness is of central importance to the Saintly, for "Saintliness" itself derives from "lovingkindness." And Chazal have said (Avos 1.2), "The world stands on three things," one of which is lovingkindness. They have numbered it (Peah 1.1) among those things whose fruits a man eats in this world and whose essence endures for his reward in the World to Come. And they have said (Sotah 14a), "R. Simlai learned, "The Torah begins and ends with lovingkindness." "Rava learned (Yevamoth 79a), `All who possess these three traits are without question of the seed of our father Abraham mercy, shyness, and lovingkindness.' " R. Eleazar said (Sukkah 49b), "Lovingkindness is greater than charity, as it is said (Hosea 10:12), `Sow for yourselves with charity and reap with lovingkindness.' " "Lovingkindness is greater than charity in three ways: Charity is performed with one's wealth, and lovingkindness with one's body; charity is given to the poor, and lovingkindness to rich and poor alike; charity is given only to the living, and lovingkindness to the living and the dead alike." And (Shabbath 151a), "'And He will give you mercy and He will have mercy upon you' (Dvarim 13:18) - Heaven is merciful to all who have mercy upon their fellow creatures." This is self-evident; for since Hashem pays measure for measure, one who is merciful toward his fellow creatures and treats them with lovingkindness is deserving of mercy and of absolution of his sins in lovingkindness. As Chazal have said (Rosh Hashanah 17a), "Whose sins does He forgive? The sins of one who overlooks an injustice committed against him." And if one is unwilling to forego his claims or to act with lovingkindness, it follows that he, too, is to be treated only in accordance with strict justice. Who could abide it if Hashem acted on the basis of justice alone? King David prayed (Tehillim 143:2), "Do not enter into judgment with your servant, for no living creature will be found righteous before You." One who engages in lovingkindness, however, will receive lovingkindness. And he will receive it in proportion to the extent that he engages in it. David exulted in possessing this good trait to the extent that he sought the good even of those who hated him (Ibid. 35:13), "When they were sick, I put on sackcloth; I tortured my soul with fasting;" and (Ibid. 7:5), "If I have paid back those who served me ill . . . "

Included in this category of Saintliness is not causing pain to any creature - even animals - and showing mercy and pity toward them. As it is stated (Mishlei 12:10), "The righteous man knows the soul of his beast." There are those who hold (Shabbath 128b) that the Torah itself prohibits the causing of pain to animals, but in any event, it is at least a Rabbinical prohibition.

In fine, mercy and beneficence must be enduringly ingrained in the heart of a Saint. His constant aim must be to give pleasure to his fellow creatures and not cause them any pain . . .

The second division of Saintliness concerns the manner of performance, which is itself divided into two sections comprising many particular instances. These two chief sections are fear and love of Hashem, the two pillars of true Divine service, without which it has no foundation at all. Included in the fear of Hashem is humbling oneself before Hashem, feeling shame in approaching Divine Service, and honoring the mitzvos, the Name and the Torah of Hashem. Included in the love of Hashem are joy, communion, and jealousy. We shall now explain each factor individually.

The chief aspect of fear of Hashem is the fear of His exalted nature. A person must be mindful, when engaged in prayer or in the performance of a mitzvah, that it is before the King of Kings that he prays or performs the deed. As the Tanna has exhorted us (Berachoth 28b), "And when you pray, know before whom you pray."

There are three things which a person must look into and consider well in order to acquire such fear. The first is that he is actually standing in the presence of the Creator, Blessed be His Name, and communicating with Him, even though He cannot be seen. This is the hardest of the three for a person to create a true picture of in his heart, for he is entirely unaided by his senses toward this objective. However, one who is possessed of sound intelligence will, with a little thought and attention, be able to implant in his heart the truth of his actually communicating with Hashem, of His imploring and entreating Him and being heard and listened to by Hashem in the same way that a man, speaking to his friend, is heard and listened to by him. After having implanted this in his mind, he must give thought to the majesty of Hashem, His being elevated and raised above all blessing and praise, above all forms of perfection that his mind can envisage and comprehend. He must also think upon the lowliness of man and upon his inferior quality, which is attributable to his earthiness and grossness and, especially, to all of the sins that he has ever committed. When he considers all of this, it will be impossible for his heart not to fear and tremble when he puts forth his words before Hashem and mentions His Name and attempts to find favor in His eyes. As it is said (Tehillim 2:11), "Serve Hashem in fear and rejoice in trembling;" and (Ibid. 89:8), "A Hashem that is mighty in the great council of the holy ones and greatly feared of all who serve Him." The angels, in that they are closer to Hashem, being unfettered by earthy bodies, may more easily envisage His greatness, and, consequently, His fear is upon them to a greater extent than it is upon human beings. King David, may Peace be upon him, would extol Hashem (Ibid. 5:8), "1 will bow down to the sanctuary of Your holiness in fear of You." And it is written (Malachi 2:5), "And he trembled before my Name," and (Ezra 9:6), "My G- d, 1 was sorely ashamed and humiliated to lift, my Hashem, my face to You." However, this type of fear must first grow in the heart before it manifests itself in the body in the form of a bowed head, a bent body, lowered eyes and the folding of one's hands as a little servant before a great king. As it is stated in the Gemara (Shabbath 10a), "Rava would fold his hands and pray, saying, `I am like a servant before his Master.' "

We have thus far spoken of humility and shame. We shall now speak of honor. Chazal have already exhorted us concerning the dignity and dearness of a miizvah (.Shabbath 133b): " `This is my Hashem and I will beautify Him' (Exodus 15:2) - beautify youself before Him with mitzvos - with beautiful tzitzith, beautiful tefillin, a beautiful Torah scroll, a beautiful lulav ..." And further (Bava Kamma 9b), "A person should expend up to an extra third for the sake of beauty in a mitzvah. Anything up to this point is paid for by him, and anything beyond it, by Hashem." It is perfectly clear from what Chazal have said that the performance of the mitzvah is not enough; it must be honored and beautified.

There are those, who to make things easier for themselves, would contend that honor is meaningful only to human beings, who are deceived by such vanities, but completely superfluous to Hashem who is above these things and unaffected by them, faithful performance of the mitzvos being enough for Him. But the truth is that Hashem Blessed be He is called "The Hashem of Honor" and we are duty-bound to accord honor to Him even though He has no need of it, it being insignificant and worthless to Him. One who is in a position to give much honor to Hashem, but does not do so, is considered a sinner. The Prophet Malachi inveighed against the Jews with the word of G -d (Malachi 1:8), "If you offer a blind animal to be sacrificed, it is not evil in your eyes. Present it to your governor. Will you find favor with him? Will he be gracious to you?" Chazal have exhorted us to conduct ourselves in quite the opposite manner in our Divine service. For example, they say (Sukkah 50a) that water which has become exposed should not be strained to render it acceptable for ritual purposes. Though such water is permitted for mundane purposes, the concept of "Present it to your governor" disqualifies it for ritual use. Though there is nothing wrong with strained water, and though it is permissible for everyday use, considerations of respect render it unacceptable for religious purposes. It is stated in the Sifrei, " `And all your choice vows' (Dvarim 12:11) - one should offer only the choicest." Cain and Abel are a case in point. Abel offered of the first-born of his sheep and of their fats, and Cain offered of the worst of the fruits of the earth, as we are told by Chazal (Bereshith Rabbah 22.5). What was the outcome? (Bereishis 4:4,5), "And Hashem gave heed to Abel and his gift, but to Cain and his gift He gave no heed." And (Malachi 1:14), "Cursed is the deceiver who has in his flock a male, but pledges and sacrifies an abomination to Hashem ... for I am a great King."

Chazal warned us very often against the cheapening of mitzvos. They said (Shabbath 14a), "One who holds a scroll of the Law which is uncovered will be buried naked" because of the cheapening of a mitzvah.

The order of offering the first fruits gives us an insight into the meaning of the beautification of a mitzvah. We learned (Bikkurim 3.3), "The ox walks before them, his horns gilded with gold, an olive wreath upon his head..." "The rich bring their first fruits in baskets of gold, and the poor in wicker baskets ..." (Ibid. 8). "There are three categories of first fruits - the first fruits themselves, the additions to the first fruits and the decorations of first fruits ... " (Ibid. 10). It is here explicitly indicated to us how much we should add to the body of a mitzvah in order to beautify it. What we see here should serve as a model for all of the other mitzvos of the Torah.

Chazal tell us (Shabbath l0a), "Rava bar R. Huna would put on beautiful clothes and pray, saying, `Beautify yourself before your Hashem, Israel (Amos 4:12).' " And in relation to "the fine clothes of her son Esau" (Bereishis 27:15), R. Shimon ben Gamliel said (Bereshith Rabbah 65:16), "1 served my father ... but when Esau served his father, he wore only regal garments." If a creature of flesh and blood is served in this manner, how much more so should one take care to be dressed respectfully when he stands to pray before the King of Kings, Hashem, and to sit before Him as one sits before a great king.

Included in this category is the honoring of Sabbaths and Festivals; for one who gives much honor to them is certainly giving pleasure thereby to his Creator, who has commanded us (Isaiah 58:13), "And you should honor it." Once the truth of its being a mitzvah to honor the Sabbath has impressed itself upon us, many means of honoring it present themselves to us. The guiding rule in this connection is that one is duty-bound to perform any action which would add to the dignity of the Sabbath. It is for this reason that the early Sages occupied themselves with preparations for the Sabbath, each in his own way (Shabbath 119a): "R. Abahu would sit on a stool of ivory and fan the fire; R. Safra would roast the head of an animal; Rava would salt a carp; R. Huna would kindle a flame; R. Papa would twist a wick; R. Chisda minced beets; Rava and R. Yosef would split wood; R. Nachman would carry things in and out of the house, saying, `If R. Ami and R. Asi were my guests, would I not perform such labors for them?"'

R. Nachman's analogy bears consideration, for it may serve us as a model. His procedure was to reflect upon how he would normally go about honoring someone, and he would honor the Sabbath in a similar manner. In this connection it is stated (Berachoth 17a), "A person should be subtle in his fear of Hashem." He must have knowledge, and be able to deduce one thing from another and create situations through which to honor his Creator, in every way that our recognition of the greatness of His dominion over us can be revealed, so that everything attributable to Him will be greatly honored by us. And considering the fact that Hashem in His great goodness, despite all of our lowliness, willed in His humility to apportion honor to us and to impart to us His holy words, we should at least honor them with all our might and show how precious they are to us. This constitutes true fear of Hashem, the fear of His grandeur, which we mentioned above. It is this fear upon which hinges the honor that leads to the love of Hashem, as we will explain later with the help of Heaven. Such is not the case with the fear of punishment, which is not the fundamental type of fear and which does not give rise to the superior qualities of these traits.

Returning to the honoring of the Sabbath, we find (Shabbath 119a) that R. Anan wore black, that is, he dressed himself in black on the eve of the Sabbath so that the honor of the Sabbath would be more pronounced upon his donningbeautiful garments for it. We see, then, that not only the positive preparations for the Sabbath, but also the creation of a negative situation which tends, by contrast, to heighten the impression of honor in relation to the Sabbath is included in the mitzvah. This is the basis for the prohibition against fixing a meal before the Sabbath, and for similar enactments.

An aspect of fearing G -d is honoring the Torah and those who study it. We learned explicitly (Avos 4.6), "One who honors the Torah is himself honored by his fellow creatures." And Chazal said (Sanhedrin 1026), "R. Yochanan said, `Why did Ahab deserve to reign twentytwo years? Because he honored the Torah, which was given with twenty-two letters, as it is said (I Kings 20:2ff ), `And he sent messengers to Ahab ... and all the desire of your eyes let them put in their hands and take. And he said to the messengers of Ben Hadad, `Tell my master, the King, `All that you sent to your servant at first, I will do, but this thing 1 will not be able to do.' What is `the desire of your eyes?' A Torah scroll." And elsewhere they said (Berachoth 18a), "One who rides from place to place should not put a Torah scroll into a sack, place the sack upon a donkey, and ride upon it, but he should carry the scroll in his lap ... " It was also forbidden (Moed Katan 25a) to sit upon a bed on which a Torah scroll lay, as it was forbidden (Eruvin 98a) to throw away sacred writings, even Halachoth and Aggadoth, and (Megillah 27a) to place copies of Prophets and Hagiographa upon copies of the Five Books of Moshe. These things were prohibited to the whole congregation of Israel and he who would be Saintly must learn from them and add to them for the honor of the Name of Hashem, his Hashem. Included in this area of Saintliness is the necessity for cleanliness and purity during occupation with words of Torah, a requirement which extends so far as to cause thinking of them in unclean places or when one's hands are unclean to be prohibited. Chazal have very often exhorted us concerning this.

In relation to those who study Torah, Scripture tells us (Leviticus 19:32), "Rise before the grey head and honor the face of the learned." This serves as the basis for the Tzaddik to accord honor to Torah scholars in every way that he can. Chazal have said (Kethuvoth 103b), "'And he will honor those who fear Hashem' (Tehillim 15:4) - this refers to Jehoshafat, King of Judah, who, when he saw a Torah scholar, would rise from his throne, embrace him, kiss him, and say to him, `My Rabbi, my Rabbi; my teacher my teacher.' " R. Zeira (Berachoth 28a), when he was fatigued with study, would place himself by the door of the House of Study to perform the mitzvah of rising for a Torah scholar.

These are all things which we have seen the Creator, may His name be blessed, to desire, and in relation to which He has revealed His supreme judgment. This being the case, one who wishes to give pleasure to his Creator will, by these means, go forward and add to his store of devices for doing what is just before Hashem.

Included in this aspect of Saintliness is honoring the synagogue and the House of Study. It is not enough that one does not conduct himself frivolously in them, but he must observe in them all forms of honor and fear in all of his ways and actions, taking care not to do there anything that he would not do in the palace of a great king.

We shall now speak of the love of Hashem and its three branches - joy , communion and jealousy. Love of Hashem consists in a person's desiring and actually lusting for the nearness of Hashem and pursuing His holiness as one pursues anything which he strongly desires. This love extends so far as to cause the mere mentioning of Hashem's Name, the reciting of His praises and the occupation with the words of His Torah and with the nature of Hashem's Divinity to be a delight and a pleasure to one, in the same manner that one who very strongly loves the wife of his youth or his only son finds joy and pleasure in merely speaking of them. As Scripture states (Jeremiah 31:19), "For when I speak of him i will strongly remember him."

There is no question that one who truly loves his Creator will not leave off serving Him for any reason whatsoever unless he is actually forced to do so, and that he will need no motivation or inducement to serve Him, but his heart will elevate and motivate him thereto unless there is some great barrier in his way. This is the exceedingly desirable trait which the early Tzaddikim, the supremely holy, were privileged to attain. As stated by King David, may Peace be upon him (Tehillim 42:2), "As a hart yearns for the waterbrooks, so does my soul yearn for You, O G- d. My soul thirsts for Hashem, for the living Hashem - when shall I come.. ?" And (Ibid. 84:3), "My soul longs and goes out for the courts of Hashem..." and (Ibid. 63:2), "My soul thirsts for You; my flesh pines for You..." All this derives from the strength of his longing for Hashem. As the Prophet says (Isaiah 26:8), "To Your Name and to Your remembrance is the lust of the soul," and (Ibid. 9), "1 long for You in the evening; as long as my spirit is within me, I will seek You." And David himself said (Tehillim 63:7), "In truth, I will remember You upon my couch; in the night watches I will think of You." He described his pleasure and delight in speaking of Hashem and in recounting His praises (Ibid. 119:47) : "I will take delight in Your mitzvos, which I love," and (Ibid. 24), "Your mitzvos, also, are my delight . . . "

It goes without saying that this love should not depend upon any extraneous factor. That is, one should love the Creator, may His Name be blessed, not because He is good to him and grants him wealth and success, but because he is naturally impelled to do so, in the same manner that a son is naturally impelled to love his father. As stated in the Posuk (Dvarim 32:6), "Is He not your Father, your Master?"

The test of this type of love comes with difficult and troubled times. As Chazal have said (Berachoth 54a), " `And you should love Hashem, Your Hashem with all your heart and with all your soul' (Dvarim 6:5) - even if He takes your soul, `and with all your might'- with all of your possessions." But in order that troubles and pressures should not act as difficulties and deterrents in the way of the love of Hashem, a person must furnish himself with two understandings, one directed to all people alike and the other to sages with depth of mind. The first understanding is that everything which proceeds from Heaven is for the good of man. The pain and pressure itself which is evil in his eyes is, in reality, true good, in the same way that a doctor's cutting of flesh or of a limb to prevent infection from spreading to the rest of the body and killing the patient is a merciful deed, with the patient's good in mind, though on the surface it may appear to be an act of cruelty. There is no fear that the patient will cease to love the doctor because of what he has done to him; to the contrary, he will love him even more. In our case, too, if a man will but consider that everything Hashem does with Him, both in relation to his body and to his possessions is for his own good, though he may not be able to perceive or understand its being so, his love will not weaken because of any pressure or pain, but, to the contrary, will grow stronger and will steadily increase.

Those with true understanding, however, do not need even this explanation, for they are entirely unmotivated by selfinterest, their sole aspiration being to magnify the honor of G- d and to give Him pleasure. The more deterrents that cross their path, making it necessary for them to give more of themselves to counteract them, the more will their hearts fortify themselves and rejoice to show the strength of their faith, just as a general, famed for his strength will always thrust himself into the heart of the battle, where a victory will serve all the more to reveal his prowess. The joy that comes with every opportunity to express the intensity of one's love is well known to every lover of flesh and blood.

We shall now discuss the three aforementioned branches of love - communion, joy and jealousy. Communion is a state in which one's heart clings so closely to Hashem that he does not strive for and is not concerned with anything outside of Him, as alluded to in Solomon's simile (Mishlei 5:19), "A beloved gazelle, full of favor; her breasts will satiate you at all times. In her love will you always wander." And in the Gemara Chazal tell us (Eruvin 546), "It was said about R. Eleazar ben Pedath that he sat and occupied himself with Torah in the upper marketplace of Sepphoris while his garment hung in the lower market place." The end of this trait is that a man be constantly united with his Creator in this manner. At the very least he will, if he loves his Creator, certainly engage in such communion during the time of his Divine service.

In Talmud Yerushalmi (Berachoth 5.1) it is stated, "Once, R. Chanina ben Dosa, while standing and praying, was bitten by a poisonous lizard, but did not interrupt his prayers. His disciples asked him, `Our Rabbi, did you not feel anything?' He answered, `I take an oath. Because my heart was intent on my prayers, I felt nothing.' "

The Torah exhorts us very often in relation to communion with Hashem: "to love Hashem with all your heart... and to cling to Him" (Dvarim 30:20), "and to Him shall you cling" (Ibid. 10:20), "And cling to Him" (Ibid. 13:5). David said (Tehillim 63:9). "My soul clings to You." All of these verses speak of one thing - the uniting of a man with Hashem to the extent that he cannot separate himself and move from Him. And Chazal have said (Bereshith Rabbah 80:7), "R. Shimon ben Lakish said, `Hashem employed three terms of love in relation to Israel, and we learn them from the episode of Shechem ben Chammor - `communion,' `longing' and `desire.' " These are essentially the principal branches of love - the yearning that I mentioned before, the clinging to G -d and the pleasure and joy derived from occupying oneself with that which is associated with the Beloved.

The second main branch of love is joy, a fundamental principle in Divine service, in relation to which David exhorted us (Tehillim 100:2), "Serve Hashem with joy; come before Him with song" and (Ibid. 68:4), "And the righteous will rejoice. They will exult before G -d and be filled with happiness." And Chazal have said (Shabbath 306), "The Divine Presence comes to rest upon one only through his rejoicing in a mitzvah." In relation to the aforementioned verse, "Serve G- d with joy," they said (Midrash Shochar Tov ad loc.), "R. Ibu said, `When you stand before him in prayer, let your heart rejoice that you are praying to a G- d without parallel.' " This is true joy - rejoicing that one has been privileged to serve the Blessed Master, who has no equal and to occupy oneself with His Torah and His mitzvos, which embody true perfection and eternal preciousness. Solomon, in his wisdom, expressed the idea thus (Song of Songs 1:4): "Draw me on; we will run after You. The King has brought me to his chambers; we will rejoice and be happy in You." The further a person is privileged to enter into the chambers of the knowledge of the greatness of Hashem, the greater is his happiness and his heart rejoices within him. And again (Tehillim 149:2), "Israel will be happy in its Maker. The sons of Zion will rejoice in their King." David, who had already reached a high plane in the cultivation of this trait, said (Ibid. 104:34), "Let my words be pleasant to Him; I will rejoice in Hashem" and (Ibid. 43:4), "And I will come to the altar of Hashem, to the Hashem who is the joy of my rejoicing and I will praise You with the harp, O Hashem" and (Ibid. 71:23), "Let my lips rejoice, for I will sing to You, and my soul which You have redeemed." His joy waxed so strong within him that his lips moved of themselves and sang upon his being engaged in the praises of Hashem - all this because of the great fervor of his soul, which was consumed in its joy before him, as he concludes, "and my soul which you have redeemed." We find that Hashem stormed against the Jews because they omitted this element in their Divine service, as it is said (Dvarim 28:47), "Because you did not serve Hashem with happiness and willingness of heart." David, seeing in the spirit with which the Jews donated toward the building of the Temple that they had already attained to this trait, prayed that it remain with them and not depart, as it is said (I Chronicles 29:17,18), "And now, Your people that are found here I have seen offering to You with joy. O Lord, Hashem of Abraham, Isaac and Israel, our fathers, preserve this eternally for the inclination of the thoughts of the heart of Your people, and set their hearts aright with You."

The third branch of the love of Hashem is jealously - being jealous for the Holy One's Name, hating His enemies and striving to humble them as much as possible so that the service of Hashem will be done and His honor magnified. As David, may Peace be upon him, said (Tehillim 139:21,23), "Will 1 not hate those who hate You, O Lord, and will .I not rebuke those who rise against You? I hate them to the limits of hatred..." Elijah said (I Kings 19:10), "I have been exceedingly jealous for Hashem of Hosts..." It was because of this jealousy for his Hashem that he attained such heights, as in the verse (Numbers 25:13), "Because he was jealous for his Hashem and brought about atonement for Israel." Chazal were very extreme in their statements (Shabbath 546) concerning those who are in a position to rebuke others for their wrongdoing but fail to do so, stating that they themselves will be judged as having committed the sin. In Midrash Eichah (1.34) it is stated, " `Her leaders were like harts' (Lamentations 1:6)just as harts, when it is hot, turn their faces one beneath the other, so the great people of the Jews saw sin and turned their faces from it. Hashem said about them, `The time will come when I will do the same to them."' It is evident that just as one who loves his friend will not tole. rate his being beaten or insulted, but will certainly rise to his defense, so one who loves the Name of Hashem will not be able to abide the desecration of His Name (Hashem forbid) and the transgression of His mitzvos. As Solomon said (Mishlei 28:7), "The deserters of Torah will praise the wicked and the observers of Torah will rebuke them." Those who praise the wicked individual in his wickedness and do not hold his misdeed up to him are deserters of Torah, who abandon it to desecration (G -d forbid) . The observers of Torah, those who strengthen themselves in strengthening Torah, will certainly rebuke them. They will not be able to contain themselves and remain still. Hashem said to Job (Job 40:11-13), "Spread out the fury of Your wrath, and see every proud man and lower him. See every proud man and humble him and stamp down the wicked beneath them. Bury them together in the earth, their faces enclosed in hiddenness." This is the intensity of the love that one who truly loves his Creator should be able to display. As it is said (Tehillim 97:10), "Those who love Hashem hate evil."

We have thus far dealt with those aspects of Saintliness concerned with the deed and with the manner of its performance. We shall now speak of intention in relation to Saintliness.

We have already discussed the performance of actions, for the sake of Heaven or not for the sake of Heaven, according to their various levels. It cannot be said that one who is motivated in his Divine service by a desire to purify his soul before his Creator so that he can come to sit in His presence together with the just and the Saintly, to see the pleasantness of Hashem, to dwell within His Sanctuary and to receive the reward of the World to Come - it cannot be said that such a person is badly motivated. On the other hand, we cannot say that his motivation is a very good one either. For as long as a person is concerned with his own good, his Divine service is also performed for his own good. The true motivation, which is common to Tzaddikim, who have exerted themselves and persevered to acquire it, is to serve solely for the purpose of magnifying and extending the honor of the Master of Blessed Name. One will serve for this end only after he has grown strong in love for Hashem, and longs and lusts for the magnification of His honor, and is pained by anything which detracts from it. He will hope that he is at least doing his part toward magnifying the honor of Hashem and he will wish that all others possessed this aspiration. The shortcomings of others in this respect will pain and grieve him, not to speak of his own unintentional and accidental lapses and those resulting from his natural weakness, which makes it difficult for him to constantly protect himself against sin, as it is stated (Ecclesiastes 7:20), "A man is not righteous in the land, who will do good and not sin."

The Saintly attitude we are discussing has been set forth in Tanna d'bei Eiiyahu (Chapter 4): "Every sage in Israel who possesses the words of Torah according to their true significance and grieves for the honor of Hashem and for the honor of Israel all his days, and lusts and feels pain for the honor of Jerusalem and of the Temple and for the swift flowering of salvation and the ingathering of the exiles, attains to the infusion of the Divine spirit in his words... " This, then, is the proper frame of mind for one to cultivate, removed as it is from all considerations of personal pleasure, directed only toward the honor of the Presence and toward the sanctification of His Name, which is sanctified by His creations when they do His will. In relation to this it is said (Zohar Mishpatim), "Who is a Tzaddik -one who is Saintly with his Creator." A Tzaddik of this kind, aside from being motivated in the proper manner in relation to the performance of mitzovth in pursuance of his Divine service, must, without doubt, constantly feel actual pain over Jerusalem and the Destruction because of their tendency to minimize the honor of Hashem, and will lust for the Redemption so that the honor of Hashem may grow. As stated by the aforementioned Tanna d'bei Eliyahu, "And he lusts and feels pain for the honor of Jerusalem and prays constantly for the Redemption of Israel and for the restoration of the honor of Heaven to its former pre-eminence." If one would say, "Who am I and what am I worth that I should pray for Jerusalem etc... Will the exiles be gathered in and will Salvation sprout because of my prayer?" his answer awaits him. As we learned (Sanhedrin 37a), "Man was created individually so that each man should say, `The world was created for my sake.' " it is Hashem's pleasure that His sons desire and pray for this. And though their desire may not be fulfilled because the proper time has not yet arrived or for some other reason, they will have done their part and Hashem rejoices in it. The Prophet stormed over the absence of this attitude (Isaiah

59:16), "And he saw that there was no man and he was amazed that there was no contender" and (Ibid. 63:5), "And I looked and there was no helper, and I was amazed and there was no supporter" and (Jeremiah 30:17), "It is Zion; no one inquires after it." Commenting upon this verse Chazal said (Sukkah 41a), "This shows that it needs inquiring after." We see, then, that we are dutybound in this respect. We cannot exempt ourselves because of our inadequate strength, for in relation to all such things we learned (Avos 2.16), "The work is not yours to complete, but you are not free to abstain from it." And the Prophet says elsewhere (Isaiah 51:18), "She has no one to lead her from among all the sons to whom she has given birth; no one to hold her hand from among all the sons she has raised." And the verse (Ibid. 40:6), "All flesh is grass and all of his kindness is as the blossoming of the field," Chazal interpreted (Avodah Zarah 2b) as meaning that all of their kindnesses are performed for their own sake, for their own good and pleasure, that they are not governed by this pure motivation and do not seek the magnification of G -d's honor and the redemption of Israel. The honor of Hashem can grow only with the redemption of Israel and the growth of their honor, the one, in reality, being dependent upon the other, as may be seen in the aforementioned Tanna d'bei Eliyahu, "And he grieves over the honor of Hashem and over the honor of Israel."

There are two considerations, then, in relation to this aspect of intention. The first is that the intention behind every mitzvah and act of Divine service be the magnification of the honor of the Presence, which derives from His creations' giving pleasure to Him, and the second that one feel pain for His honor, and long that it be perfectly magnified through the magnification of Israel's honor and through their well-being.

The second aspect of intention concerns the good of the generation. It befits every Tzaddik to be motivated in his actions by a concern for the good of the entire generation, a desire to benefit and protect them. This is the intent of the verse (Isaiah 3:10), "Praise the righteous for he is good; for they eat the fruits of their deeds." The whole generation eats of their fruits. Our sages have commented similarly (Bava Bathra 15a), " `Does it contain trees? ' (Numbers 13:20) - is anyone there who shelters his generation as a tree?" We see it to be the will of the Presence that the Tzaddikim of Israel benefit and atone for all of the other levels within the nation, as Chazal intimated in their statement concerning the lulav and its accompanying species (Vayikra Rabbah 30.12), "Let these come and atone for those." For Hashem does not desire the destruction of the wicked; it is rather a mitzvah devolving upon the Tzaddik to benefit and atone for them. This intention must be contained in his Divine service and it must manifest itself in his prayers; that is, he must pray on behalf of his generation to seek atonement for him who needs atonement, to turn to repentance him who requires it, and to speak in defense of his entire generation. Chazal tell us (Ein Yaakov Yoma Ch. 8) in relation to the verse Daniel 10:12), "And I have come with your words," that Gabriel did not return within the Divine Curtain until he had defended Israel. And about Gideon it is said (Yalkut), "Go with this, your strength" (Judges 6:14), the strength of his having defended his people. Hashem loves only him who loves Israel; and to the extent that one's love for Israel grows, to that extent does the love of Hashem grow for him. These are the true shepherds of Israel whom Hashem greatly desires, who sacrifice themselves for His sheep, who concern themselves with their peace and well-being, and exert themselves for it in every way possible, who always stand in the breach to pray for them, to nullify stern decrees and to open the gates of blessing for them. The situation is analogous to that of a father, who loves no man more than the one whom he sees to have a genuine love for his sons. Human nature attests to this. And this is the idea behind the statement concerning the High Priests (Makkoth lla), "They should have pleaded for mercy on behalf of their generation, but failed to do so, " and behind the statement (Ibid.), "A man was eaten by a lion at a distance of three miles from R. Joshua ben Levi and Elijah did not appear to him for three days." We see, then, that it is the Saint's duty to seek the good of his generation and to exert himself for it.

We have now explained the chief divisions of Saintliness. It is for each man of intelligence and for each pure heart to deal with particular instances, to conduct himself justly in relation to them, each in its own time, according to the principles here set forth.

CHAPTER XX

CONCERNING THE WEIGHING OF SAINTLINESS

WHAT MUST Now be explained is the weighing of one's deeds in relation to the aforementioned standards of Saintliness. This is an extremely fundamental process and one which constitutes the most difficult operation in Saintliness because of the great subtlety it demands and because of its susceptibility to great inroads by the evil inclination. The weighing of Saintliness entails great danger because it is within the power of the evil inclination to draw many good things far from one, as if they were evil and to draw many sins near to him, as if they were great mitzvos. The truth is that a man must fulfill three requirements in order to succeed in this "weighing." He must possess the most just of hearts, whose only inclination is to give pleasure to Hashem; he must submit his actions to the closest scrutiny and exert himself to perfect them in accordance with this end; and after all this, he must cast his lot with Hashem, after which it may be said of him (Tehillim 84:6,12), "Happy is the man whose strength is in You ... Goodness will not be lacking for those who walk in purity." if one of these conditions is not observed, he will not attain to Wholeness and he will be very apt to stumble and fall. That is, if his intention is not select and pure, or if he weakens in the analysis of his deeds so that his full potential is not brought to bear upon them, or, if after all .this, he does not put his trust in his Master, it will be very difficult for him not to fall. But if he correctly observes all three - purity of thought, analysis, and trust, he will walk securely in truth and no evil will befall him, as Channah said in her prophecy (I Samuel 2:9), "He will protect the feet of his Tzaddikim." And David also said (Tehillim 37:28), "And He will not forsake his Tzaddikim; they will forever be protected."

What must be understood is that actions should not be judged for saintliness at first glance, but should be carefully observed and reflected upon so that it may be determined how far their results extend. For at times an action in itself may seem worthy of performance, but because its results are evil, one will be obliged to leave it; and if he does not, he will be adjudged a sinner rather than a Saint. The episode of Gedaliah ben Achikam (Jeremiah 40:13ff) provides a clear illustration of this fact. Because of his abundant Saintliness, which would not permit him to judge Yishmael adversely, or which would not permit him to receive slander, he said to Yochanan ben Kareach, "You are speaking falsely of Yishmael." What was the result? He died, the Jews were scattered, and their last hope was extinguished. And Scripture attributes to him the death of those people who were killed, as if he were the murderer, as indicated by the comment of Chazal upon the verse, (Jeremiah 41:9), "All of the corpses of the people who were killed through Gedaliah."

It was also such incorrectly weighed Saintliness in the incident of Bar Kamtza (Gittin 56a) that was responsible for the destruction of the Temple: "The Rabbis thought to sacrifice the animal. R. Zechariah ben Avkulos said to them, `They will say that animals with imperfections may be sacrificed upon the altar.' The Rabbis thought to kill him [Bar Kamtza]. R. Zachariah ben Avkulos said to them, `They will say that one who causes an imperfection in sacrificial animals should be killed.' While all this was going on, the evildoer slandered the Jews to the emperor, who came and destroyed Jerusalem." It was to this that R. Yochanan was referring when he said, "The humility of R. Zechariah destroyed our Temple, consumed our Sanctuary and exiled us among the nations."

We see, then, that one should not decide upon the saintliness of a deed on the basis of surface appearances, but should view it from every angle that human intelligence can be brought to bear upon it, until he can truthfully determine the better course - performance or abandonment.

For example, the Torah commanded us (Leviticus 19:16), "Rebuke your friend firmly." Very often a man will undertake to rebuke sinners in such a place or at such a time that he will cause them to go even further in their wickedness and to add to their sins by desecrating the Name of Hashem. In such cases, silence alone constitutes Saintliness. As Chazal have said (Yevamoth 656), "Just as it :s a mitzvah to say what will be listened to, so is it a mitzvah not to say what will not be listened to." It goes without saying that one should attempt to be in the forefront in the pursuit of mitzvos and to be among those who occupy themselves with them. But sometimes this may lead to quarrels, which might result more in shame to the mitzvah and desecration of the Name of Heaven than in honor. In situations of this kind the Tzaddik is certainly required to leave the mitzvah and not pursue it. As Chazal have stated in relation to the Levites (Bamidbar Rabbah 5.1), "Because they knew that the reward of those who carried the ark was greater, they abandoned the table, the candlestick and the altars, and they all ran to the ark to receive reward. This resulted in quarrels - one saying, `I will carry here' and the other saying, `1 will carry here.' This, in turn, led to frivolity, and the Divine Presence assailed them..."

Again, a man must observe all of the mitzvos with all of their fine points without fear or shame, no matter in whose presence he finds himself, as it is stated (Tehillim 119:46), "And I will speak of Your testimonies before kings and I will not be ashamed" and (Avos 5:23), "Be strong as a leopard ..." But this, too, requires distinction and discrimination, for all this was said in relation to the mitzvah in itself, for whose sake one must set his face like flint. But there are some additions to Saintliness which, if a man will perform them in public, will cause people to laugh at and ridicule him, rendering them sinners and liable to punishment because of him. Because he can forego these actions, their not being absolutely required, the Tzaddik would certainly do better to leave them than to do them. And the Prophet said (Micha 6:8), "And walk modestly with your G -d." Many great Tzaddikim left off some of their accustomed ways of Saintliness when in public so as not to appear proud. In fine, what is essential in respect to mitzvos must be performed in the face of all mockery, and what is not essential and provokes laughter and ridicule should not be performed.

We see, then, that one who would be a true Tzaddik must weigh all of his deeds in relation to their results and in relation to all of the circumstances surrounding their performance - time, social environment, situation and place. And if he finds that not doing will go farther toward sanctifying the Name of Heaven and giving pleasure to Hashem than doing, he must refrain from doing. Or, if one action appears good, but is bad in its results or in its complements, and another appears bad, but is good in its results, he must decide on the basis of the conclusion and the result, the true fruit of the action. This decision is left to an understanding heart and an honest intelligence, for, in view of their innumerability, it is impossible to consider particular instances. "Hashem gives wisdom; from His mouth stems knowledge and understanding" (Mishlei 2:6).

The episode of R. Tarfon (Berachoth 10b) substantiates what has been said. Although he took upon himself the more stringent decision of Beth Shammai, he was told, "You would rightly have been accounted the cause of your own death, for you violated the words of Beth Hillel." All this because the controversy between Beth Shammai and Beth Hillel had become an area of difficulty to Israel in view of the great contention that had grown up between them; and after it had finally been ruled that the law should constantly be decided in accordance with Beth Hillel it was essential for the very endurance of Torah that this ruling forever retain its force and not be weakened in any way lest the Torah come to take on the semblance of two Torahs (Hashem forbid). Hence, the view of this Mishnah that it is Saintlier to hold with Beth Hillel even when more lenient, than to be more stringent in accordance with Beth Shammai. This should serve us as a guide to perceive the path where light resides with truth and faith for the doing of what is just in the eyes of Hashem.

CHAPTER XXI

CONCERNING THE MEANS OF ACQUIRING SAINTLINESS

WHAT IS VERY INSTRUMENTAL in the acquisition of Saintliness is much observation and thought. For when a person expends much thought upon the greatness of Hashem's majesty, upon His absolute perfection, and upon the infinitely great gap between His sublimity and our lowliness, he will be filled with fear and tremble before Him. And in thinking upon His great lovingkindness to us, upon the strength of Hashem's love for man, upon the nearness of the just to Him, and upon the nobility of Torah and mitzvos - in thinking upon these and upon similar ideas, he will certainly be fired with a strong love for Hashem and will choose and lust to be united with Him. For when he sees that Hashem is actually a Father to us and pities us as a father pities his sons, he will naturally be awakened with a desire and a longing to reciprocate to Him, as a son to his father. But to acquire this attitude, he must closet himself and gather all of his knowledge and thought for consideration and study of the truths that we have mentioned. He will certainly be aided in this by much preoccupation with and close application to the Tehillim of David, may Peace be upon him, and by reflection upon their statements and ideas. For since the Tehillim are all filled with the love and fear of Hashem and with all types of Saintliness, in thinking upon them he cannot but be greatly inspired to follow in the Psalmist's footsteps and to walk in his ways. Also helpful is the reading of those works which deal with incidents in the lives of the Tzaddikim, for these incidents stimulate the intelligence to take counsel and to imitate the Saint's worthy deeds. This is evident.

The deterrents to Saintliness are preoccupation and worries. When one's intelligence is preoccupied and pressed with his worries and his affairs, it cannot turn to the thoughts we have spoken of; and without reflection Saintliness cannot be attained. And even if one has already attained it, preoccupations exert pressure upon his intelligence and confuse it and do not permit him to strengthen himself in fear and love and in the other aforementioned aspects of Saintliness. This is the intent behind the statement of Chazal (Shabbath 30b), "The Divine Presence does not reside in the midst of sadness ..."

What we have said holds especially true of enjoyments and pleasures, which are diametrically opposed to Saintliness, for they induce the heart to be pulled along after them and to depart from all aspects of Separation and true knowledge. However, a man can be protected against these deterrents and rescued from them by trusting to Hashem, by casting his lot with Him in the realization that a person can never be deprived of what has been set aside for him, as Chazal have said (Beitzah 16a), "A man's entire sustenance is determined for him on Rosh Hashana ..." and (Yoma 38b), "A man cannot touch even a hairsbreadth of what has been set aside for his neighbor." A man could sit idle and what was ordained for him would materialize, were it not for the penalty imposed upon all men: "With the sweat of your brow shall you eat bread" (Bereishis 3:19), because of which, by Divine decree, a man is required to exert himself somewhat for his sustenance. This is a tax, as it were, which must be paid by every member of the human race and which cannot be evaded. In the words of Chazal (Sifrei), "I would think that a man would be permitted to sit idle, had we not been told (Dvarim 28:20), `With all the putting forth of your hand which you undertake.' " This is not to say that the exertion produces the results, but that it is necessary. Once one has exerted himself, however, he has fulfilled his responsibilities and made room for the blessing of Heaven to rest upon him, and he need not consume his days in striving and exertion. As King David, may Peace be upon him, said (Tehillim 75:7,8), "For not from east or west and not from the wilderness comes uplifting. This one He puts down and this one He lifts up. For Hashem rules." And King Solomon, may Peace be upon him, said (Mishlei 23:4), "Do not weary yourself to become rich; cease from your understanding." The correct approach in this area is that of the early Tzaddikim, who made their Torah primary and their labor secondary, and were successful in both; for once a man does a little work, from then on he need only trust in his Master and not be troubled by any wordly matters. His mind will then be free and his heart ready for true Saintliness and pure Divine service.

CHAPTER XXII

CONCERNING THE TRAIT OF HUMILITY

WE HAVE ALREADY discussed the shamefulness of pride and have been made aware, by inference, of the praiseworthiness of Humility. We shall now discuss Humility directly, and the nature of pride will become clear of itself.

The essence of Humility is in a person's not attaching importance to himself for any reason whatsoever. This trait is the very opposite of pride and its results are the very opposite of the results of pride. Analysis will reveal that Humility is dependent upon thought and deed. Before a man conducts himself in the way of the Humble, he must first be Humble in thought. One who attempts to be Humble in deeds without first having cultivated an attitude of Humility belongs to that class of wicked, deceitful, "humble" people which we mentioned previously, that class of hypocrites, than which there is nothing more evil in the world.

We shall now explain these divisions.

Humility in thought consists in a person's reflecting upon and recognizing as a truth the fact that he does not deserve praise and honor (let alone elevation above his fellow men), both because of his natural limitations and because of his accumulated defects. As far as natural limitations are concerned, it is obvious that it is impossible for any man, regardless of the level of perfection he has reached, to be without many faults, whether because of his own nature, because of his family and relatives, because of certain experiences he has had, or because of his deeds. ("For a man is not righteous in the land who will do good..." [Ecclesiastes 7:20]) All of these are defects in a person which allow no room at all for the feeling of self-importance; for though he may possess many virtues, these faults suffice to overshadow them.

The factor that is responsible more than any other for a person's coming to feel self-important and proud is wisdom. This is so because wisdom is a superior quality of the person himself, a function of his most honored faculty, intelligence. But there is no sage who will not err and will not need to learn from the words of his friends and, very often, even from those of his disciples. How, then, can he pride himself in his wisdom? In truth, one who is possessed of an honest intelligence, even if he has managed to become a toweringly great sage, will see, when he looks into the matter, that there is no room at all for pride and self-importance. For a man of intelligence, one who knows more than others, acts only according to the dictates of his nature, as it is natural for a bird to fly, and as it is dictated for an ox to pull with his strength. One is wise only because his nature has led him to be so. And one who is not so wise now, were he in possession of the sage's natural intelligence, would become just as wise as he. There is no place, then, for self-importance and pride in respect to wisdom. Rather, if one possesses much wisdom, he is duty-bound to impart it to those in need of it. As stated by R. Yochanan ben Zakkai (Avos 2.9), "If you have learned much Torah, do not take credit for it, for you were created to do so." One who is wealthy may rejoice in his lot, but at the same time he must help those in need. If one is strong, he must assist the weak and rescue the oppressed. The situation is analogous to that of a household where there are different servants assigned to different tasks, and where each servant must fulfill his appointed task if the affairs and requirements of the household are all to be attended to. In truth there is no place for pride here.

This is the type of analysis and reflection that should be engaged in by every man of honest, unperverted intelligence. And when this idea becomes clear to him, he will be reckoned the truly Humble man, Humble in his heart and in his very being. As David said to Michael (II Samuel 6:22), "And I was lowly in my eyes." And as Chazal have said (Sotah 56), "How great are the Humble in spirit! In the time of the Temple if one sacrificed a burnt-offering, he was accredited with a burnt-offering; if he sacrificed a meal-offering, he was accredited with a meal-offering. But if one possesses a Humble spirit it is considered in the Posuk as if he had offered all of the sacrifices, as it is said (Tehillim 51:19), `The sacrifices of Hashem are a broken spirit.' " This is the praise of the lowly in spirit, the Humble in heart and in thought. Elsewhere it is said (Chullin 89a), " `Not because you are more numerous than the other nations' (Dvarim 7:7) - Hashem said to Israel, `My sons, I desire you because even when I impart greatness to you, you demean yourselves before Me. I gave greatness to Abraham and he said (Bereishis 18:27), `And I am dust and ashes.' I gave greatness to Moshe and Aaron and they said (Exodus 16:7), `What are we?' I gave greatness to David and he said (Tehillim 22:7), `And I am a worm and not a man.'" All this because the man with an honest heart does not permit himself to be deceived by any virtue that he might possess, knowing the truth - that he does not thereby emerge from his lowliness, because of all of the faults that he must perforce possess. He realizes, too, that even in relation to those mitzvos which he has attained he has not arrived at the ultimate goal. And he is aware that even if he possessed no other shortcoming than that of being flesh and blood, being born of woman, it would be more than enough to render him so lowly and inferior as to cause the feeling of sell-importance to be completely unbefitting him; for every virtue that he attains represents nothing more than Hashem's lovingkindness to him, G- d's desire to be gracious to him, in spite of the fact that in point of his nature and his earthiness he is extremely lowly and shameful. His reaction, then, should be to thank Him who has been so gracious, and to constantly grow in Humility.

The situation is analogous to that of a pauper who accepts the gifts of kindness and cannot help but be ashamed because of them. The more kindness he receives the greater grows his shame. The similarity in situations will be perceived by anyone whose eyes are open enough to see himself as attaining virtues through Hashem. As King David said (Tehillim 116:12), "What can I return to G -d for all of his lovingkindness to me?" We are acquainted with instances of great Tzaddikim who were punished because, with all of their Saintliness, they took credit for themselves. In relation to Nehemiah ben Chachaliah Chazal said (Sanhedrin 936), "Why was his work not called by his name? Because he took credit for himself." And Hezekiah said (Isaiah 38:17), "Peace is very bitter for me," because Hashem had answered him (Ibid. 37:35), "And I will protect this city. I will come to its aid for my sake and for the sake of David, my servant." As Chazal say (Berachoth 10b), "That which one attributes to his own merit will be attributed to the merit of another." We see, then, that a man should not even take credit for the good things he has done, let alone become self-important and proud because of them.

But, in truth, all that we have said is intended for those who are like Abraham, Moshe, Aaron and David and the other Tzaddikim that we have mentioned, but we, who are orphans of orphans, do not need all this, for we, have so many faults that we need not engage in much analysis to see our lowliness and to realize that all of our wisdom is of no account.

The greatest sage among us is no more than the disciple of the disciples of the early generations. It would do for us to understand and acknowledge this truth so that our hearts do not swell in vain. Let us recognize that our minds are insubstantial and our intelligence very weak, that we are very ignorant and very much subject to error, and that what knowledge we do possess is extremely minute. This being the case, there should certainly be no room in a person's feelings for self-importance, but only for shame and lowliness. This is self-evident.

We have thus far spoken of Humility of thought. We shall now speak of Humility of deed. This latter area is divided into four parts: conducting oneself with lowliness, bearing insults, hating authority and fleeing honor, and apportioning honor to all men.

Conducting oneself with lowliness: This applies to one's manner of speaking, walking and sitting, and to all of one's movements. In relation to one's speech Chazal have said (Yoma 86a), "A man should always speak gently with his fellow men." And Scripture explicitly states (Ecclesiastes 9:17), "The words of the wise, spoken gently, are accepted." One's words must be words of honor and not words of shame, as it is said (Mishlei 11:12), "One who shames his friend is lacking a heart," and (Ibid. 18:3), "When the wicked man comes, there also comes shame."

In relation to one's manner of walking Chazal said (Sanhedrin 88b), "They sent from the Holy Land, `Who will inherit the World to Come? A humble man, whose knee is low, who is bent coming in and bent going out.' " One should not walk erect, nor in a formalized, mincing manner, but as one going about his tasks. Chazal have said (Kiddushin 31a), "If one walks erect it is as if he pushes the feet of the Divine Presence." And it is written (Isaiah 10:33), "Those of great stature will be cut down."

As far as one's manner of sitting is concerned, a person should see to it that his place is among the lowly and not among the high. In this, too, Scripture is explicit (Mishlei 25:6), "Do not glorify yourself before a king and do not stand in the place of the great . . ." Along the same lines, Chazal said in Vayikra Rabbah (1.5), "Withdraw two or three levels from your place so that they will say to you, `Come forward,' rather than go forward and be told, `Get back.' " And concerning those who belittle themselves they said (Bava Metzia 85b), "All who belittle themselves for the sake of Torah in this world are elevated in the World to Come." They added further (Yalkut Ezekiel 361), " `Remove the turban and lift off the crown' (Ezekiel 21:31) - all who are great in this world are small in the World to Come;" and, conversely, if one is small in this world, his time of greatness is in the World to Come. Elsewhere they said (Sotah 5a), "A man should learn from the example set by his Master. Hashem bypassed all the mountains and hills, and caused his Divine Presence to come to rest upon Mount Sinai." This because of its lowliness. And (Rosh Hashanah 17a), " `To the remnant of His inheritance' (Micah 7:18) - to those who act as if they considered themselves remnants."

Bearing insults: Chazal have explicitly stated (Ibid.), "Whose sins does He forgive? The sins of those who overlook the wrong committed against them." And (Shabbath 886), "Concerning those who are insulted but do not insult in return, who are shamed, but do not shame in return, it is said (Judges 5:31), `His lovers are like the emerging of the sun in its strength.' " They told of the great Humility of Bava ben Buta (Nedarim 666): "A Babylonian went up to Israel and got married. One time he said to his wife, `Cook for me ... Go and break them over the head of the door.' While Bava ben Buta was sitting in judgment, she, having mistaken her husband's meaning, broke them over his head. He asked her, `Why have you done this?' and she answered, `My husband told me to.' He said, `You did the will of your husband. May the Presence bring forth from you two sons like Bava ben Buta.' " They spoke likewise of the great Humility of Hillel (Shabbath 30b), "Our Rabbis learned, `One should always be humble in the manner of Hillel. . .' " And R. Abahu, with all of his Humility, found that he was not yet worthy of being considered Humble (Sotah 40a) : "R. Abahu said, "At first I though I was Humble, but when I saw that R. Abba of Akko gave one reason and his interpreter another, and he still did not become angry. I said to myself, `I am not humble."'

Hating authority and fleeing honor are explicitly treated in the Mishnah (Avos 1.10) : "Love labor and hate authority." (Ibid. 4.9), "One whose heart swells in his handing out of legal decisions is foolish, wicked and haughty." (Eruvin 13b), "If one pursues honor, honor flees from him." (Pesikta Rabbathi), " `Do not be quick to enter into controversy' (Mishlei 28:8) - do not pursue authority, for what will you do afterwards? The next day they will come and put questions to you. How will you answer them?" "R. Menachama in the name of R. Tanchum said, `All who accept positions of authority for their personal satisfaction are like adulterers who derive enjoyment from the body of a woman.' " "R. Abahu said, `I [Hashem] am called "holy"; if you do not possess all of My traits, do not assume authority.' " The incident of the disciples of Rabbi Gamliel bears out this idea. Although they were sorely pressed by their poverty, they declined positions of authority. In the words of Chazal (Horioth 10a), "Do you think I give you lordship? I give you servitude... " And (Pesachim 87b), "Woe to lordship, which buries its possessors." How do we know this? Through Joseph, who, because he conducted himself authoritatively, died before his brothers (Berachoth 55a).

In sum, authority is only a great burden upon the shoulders of those who bear it; for as long as a man is alone, dwelling in the midst of his nation, just one among many, he is held responsible only for himself, but once he ascends to lordship and authority he is held responsible for all who come within his authority and jurisdiction. He must look to the welfare of all of them, lead them with knowledge and intelligence, and set their actions aright. And if he does not do so, he comes, according to Chazal (Devarim Rabbah 1.10) within the province of "And their guilt is on your heads" (Dvarim 1:13). Honor is nothing but the vanity of vanities, which causes a man to defy his own mind and that of his Master and to forget his entire duty. One who recognizes it for what it is will certainly find it despicable and will hate it. The praise of people will be a burden to him, for when he sees people heaping praises upon him for qualities he does not even possess, he will only be ashamed and will grieve, feeling that it is not bad enough that he does not possess the virtues he is being praised for, but people must add to his shame by praising him falsely. Apportioning honor to all men: We have learned (Avos 4.1), "Who is honored? One who honors his fellow-men." They said further, "How do we know that one must accord honor to his neighbor if he knows him to be greater than himself in even one respect ... (Pesachim 113b). "Hasten to greet every man" (Avos 4:15), It was said (Berachoth 17a) about R. Yochanan ben Zakkai that no man ever preceded him in the pronunciation of the greeting, even a gentile in the market place." One must act with honor toward his neighbors, both in word and deed. Chazal

(Yevamoth 62b) have told of the twenty-four thousand disciples of R. Akiva who died because they did not accord honor to each other.

Just as shame is identified with the wicked, as seen in the aforementioned verse (Mishlei 18:3), "When the wicked man comes, there also comes shame," so is honor identified with the righteous. Honor dwells with them and does not separate itself from them, as Scripture states (Isaiah 24:23), "And before His elders there is honor."

The chief divisions of Humility have been explained. Decisions in relation to particular instances, as in all such cases, are subject to considerations of situation, time and place. "Let the wise man listen and add to his understanding" (Mishlei 1 :5).

Unquestionably, Humility removes many stumbling blocks from a man's path and brings him near to many good things; for the Humble man is little concerned with wordly affairs and is not moved to envy by its vanities. Furthermore, his company is very pleasant and he gives pleasure to his fellowmen. He is perforce never aroused to anger and to controversy; he does everything quietly and calmly. Happy are those who have been privileged to attain this trait! Chazal have said (Yerushalmi Shabbath 1.3), "That which wisdom made a wreath for its head, Humility made a heel for its sandal." All of wisdom cannot approach it. This is clear.

CHAPTER XXIII

CONCERNING THE MEANS OF ACQUIRING HUMILITY

THERE ARE TWO FACTORS which bring a person to Humility: habit and thought. Habit, in this respect, consists in a person's accustoming himself little by little to Humility by conducting himself with lowliness after the fashion previously mentioned - occupying a humble seat, walking at the end of the company, and wearing modest garments (respectable but not showy). By accustoming himself to this mode of conduct, he will cause Humility to enter into his heart and to inhabit it little by little until it has securely imbedded itself there. For since it is a person's nature to swell with self-importance, it is difficult to root out this inclination at its source. It is only through outward actions, which are under his control, that he can affect his inner self, which is not to a similar extent subject to his direction, as we explained in relation to Zeal. All of this is contained in the statement of Chazal (Berachoth 17a), "A man should always be subtle in his fear of Hashem;" that is, he should seek devices by which to counteract his nature and its inclination until he is victorious over them.

Thought in respect to the acquisition of Humility resolves itself into several considerations. The first is ,contained in the words of Akavia ben Mahalalel (Avos 3.1), "Know whence you come - from a putrid drop; and where you are going - to a place of dust, worms and maggots; and before whom you are destined to give an accounting - before the King of Kings, Hashem." In truth, all of these thoughts counteract pride and promote Humility. When a man regards the lowliness of his earthly nature and his inferior beginnings, he has no reason to feel self-important at all, but to be ashamed and degraded. The situation is analogous to that of a swineherd who has attained lordship. As long as he remembers his early days it will be impossible for him to become proud. If one considers also that after all of his greatness he will return to the earth to be food for maggots, it is certain that his pride will be humbled and his grandeur forgotten. For what is his good and his greatness if the end is shame and disgrace? And if he will reflect further and picture the moment of his entering the great court of the heavenly host, seeing himself in the presence of the King of Kings, Hashem, holy and pure to the limits of holiness and purity, in the midst of holy ones, servants of strength, strong in power, doing His bidding, entirely free of imperfection - and he standing before them, deficient, lowly and shameful in point of his nature; unclean and ugly in point of his actions -will he be able to raise his head, to open his mouth? And if he is asked, "Where then is your mouth? Where is the pride and honor that you knew in your world?" what will he answer? How will he meet this rebuke? There is no question that if a person would for one moment form a true, forceful impression of this idea, all pride would take flight from him, never to return.

The second consideration that should be reflected upon for the purpose of acquiring Humility is the variation of circumstances that is produced by time and the many changes to which it gives rise. The rich may easily become poor; the rulers, servants; and the honored, insignificant. If one can so easily be reduced to a condition which he finds so shameful today, how can he feel pride in his own condition, with which he cannot be secure? How many different kinds of sicknesses (Hashem forbid) is a person prone to, which could make it necessary for him to beg others for help and assistance, for a little relief? How many afflictions (Hashem forbid) may visit him, which could cause him to seek out many whom he formerly disdained to greet in order to gain their help. We see these things with our own eyes every day. They should serve to remove a man's pride from his heart and to clothe him in humility and lowliness.

And if a person thinks further into his duty in relation to Hashem and considers how much he forsakes it and how weak he is in its performance, he will certainly be ashamed and not proud. He will feel degraded and his heart will not swell. As stated in the Posuk (Jeremiah 31 :17,18), "I have heard Ephraim lamenting . .. `For after I repented I knew regret, and after I understood, I smote my thighs. I felt ashamed and degraded ... " Above all, one should constantly reflect upon the weakness of human intelligence and the many errors and deceits to which it is subject, upon its always being closer to error than to true understanding. He should constantly be in fear, then, of this danger and seek to learn from all men; he should give ear to advice lest he go astray. As Chazal have said (Avos 4.1), "Who is wise? One who learns from all men." And it is stated (Mishlei 12:15), "One who gives ear to advice is wise."

Among the deterrents to Humility are an abundance of the goods of this world and satiation with them; as Scripture explicitly states (Dvarim 8:12), "Lest you eat and become satiated . ..

And your heart be uplifted. .." It is for this reason that the Tzaddikim found it beneficial for a man to afflict himself at intervals - to suppress the inclination to pride, which grows strong only through abundance. As Chazal have said (Berachoth 32a), "A lion does not roar over a basket of straw, but over a basket of meat."

Heading the list of deterrents are ignorance and insufficiency of true understanding. It is to be observed that pride is most prevalent among the more ignorant. Chazal have said (Sanhedrin 24a), "A sign of pride is poverty of Torah" and (Zohar Balak), "A sign of complete ignorance is self-praise" and (Bava Metzia 856), "One coin in a pitcher makes a great deal of noise" and (Bereshith Rabbah 16.3), "The barren trees were asked `Why are your voices heard?' and they answered, `So that at least our voices might be heard and remembered.' " We have seen that Moshe, the choicest of men, was the humblest of all men.

Another deterrent to Humility is keeping company with or being served by flatterers, who, to steal a person's heart with their flattery so that he will be of benefit to them, will praise and exalt him by magnifying to their very limits the virtues that he does possess and by attributing to him virtues that he does not possess, his attributes sometimes being the very opposite of those he is being praised for. And since, in the last analysis, a person's understanding is insubstantial and his nature weak, so that he is easily deceived (especially by something toward which his nature inclines), when he hears these words being uttered by someone he has faith in, they enter into him like poison and he falls into the net of pride and is broken. A case in point is that of Yoash, who acted virtuously all the days that he was taught by Yehoyada Hakohen, his mentor (II Kings 12:3). When Yehoyada died, Yoash's servants came and began to flatter him and to magnify his virtues until, after they had virtually deified him, he gave heed to them. It is to be clearly seen that most officers and kings, and people in a position of influence in general, regardless of their level, stumble, and are corrupted by the flattery of their subordinates.

One whose eyes are open will, therefore, exercise more care and vigilance in relation to the actions of one he would choose as his friend or advisor or as the overseer of his household than he would in relation to his food and drink. For food and drink can injure one's body alone, whereas companions and overseers can destroy his soul, his might and all of his honor. King David, may Peace be upon him, said (Tehillim 101:6,7), "One who walks uprightly, he will serve me. A deceiver will not dwell within my house ..." A person's good, then, is to seek honest friends, who will open his eyes to what he is blind to and rebuke him with love in order to rescue him from all evil. For what a man cannot see because of his natural blindness to his own faults, they will see and understand. They will caution him and he will be protected. Concerning this it is said (Mishlei 24:6), "There is salvation in much counsel."

CHAPTER XXIV

CONCERNING THE FEAR OF SIN

OUR SEEING that this trait comes after all of the worthy traits heretofore mentioned is enough to awaken us to its great nobility, its integral significance and the difficulty of its attainment; for it can be attained only by one who has already acquired all of the previously mentioned traits.

At the outset it should be stated that there are two types of fear, which resolve themselves into three types. The first type is very easy to attain; there is nothing easier. The second is the most difficult of attainment, and perfection in it is, accordingly, of a very high order. The first type is fear of punishment and the second, fear of Divine Majesty, of which fear of sin is a part. We shall now explain these types of fear and their differences.

Fear of punishment, as the words imply, consists in a person's being afraid of violating Hashem's commands, because of the punishmer+ to body or soul which is meted out for transgressions. This type of fear is certainly easy to attain, for every man loves himself and fears for his soul; and there is nothing more effectual in withdrawing one from an action than the fear that it might harm him in some way. But this type of fear befits only the ignorant and women, who lack sufficient strength of mind; it is not the fear of sages and of people of understanding.

The second type of fear, fear of Divine Majesty, consists in one's withdrawing himself and abstaining from sin because of the great honor of Hashem. For how can a lowly, despicable heart of flesh and blood permit and abide the doing of what is opposed to the will of the Creator of blessed and exalted Name? This type of fear is not very easily attained, for it is born only of the knowledge and intelligence which go into reflection upon the majesty of Hashem and the lowliness of man. It is born only of the activities of the understanding, insightful mind. It is this type of fear which was classified as the second half of one of the divisions of Saintliness which we discussed earlier. One who experiences it will feel shame and will tremble in standing before his Master to pray or in performing an act of Divine service. This is the extremely worthy type of fear in which the great Tzaddikim distinguished themselves. As stated by Moshe (Dvarim 28:58), "To fear this honored, Awesome Name, Hashem, your Hashem."

The fear of sin which we are here concerned with is, in one respect, part of the fear of Divine Majesty mentioned above, and, in another, a distinct entity. It consists in a person's constantly fearing and worrying that some trace of sin might have intruded itself into his actions or that they contain something, small or great, which is inconsonant with the grandeur of Hashem's honor and with the majesty of His Name. Here we see the strong relationship between fear of sin and fear of Divine Majesty - their common concern being that one do nothing in opposition to the great Majesty of Hashem. There is a distinction between them, however, which sets the fear of sin apart and gives it its distinct name : The fear of Divine Majesty obtains only during the performance of a deed, during Divine service, or upon the materialization of an opportunity for transgression. That is, when one is standing in prayer or engaging in Divine service, he should feel ashamed and degraded; he should quake and tremble before the supreme Majesty of Hashem. Or, when an opportunity for transgression presents itself to him, and he recognizes it as such, he must keep himself from sinning so that nothing be done contrary to the honor of Hashem (Hashem forbid). The fear of sin, however, obtains at all periods and times. At every moment one must be afraid of going astray and doing something or part of a thing in opposition to the honor of Hashem's Name. Hence, the expression "fear of sin," the essence of the fear being that sin not enter into and involve itself in one's actions, whether through an intentional act, weakness, oversight or any other means. In relation to this it is said (Mishlei 28:14), "Happy is the man who fears always," which Chazal interpreted (Berachoth 60a) as referring to matters of Torah. Even when one does not see a stumbling block before him, his heart must tremble within him for fear that he is threatened by one hidden at his feet. About such fear, Moshe our Teacher, may Peace be upon him, said (Exodus 20:17), "And so that His fear be upon your faces, that you not sin." This is the central element in fear - that a person constantly fear and tremble until the fear can no longer depart from him. In this manner he will certainly avoid sin, and any sin that he might commit will be accounted accidental. Isaiah said in his prophecy (Isaiah 66:2), "And to such shall I look - to the poor, to the broken in spirit and to those who tremble at my word." King David exulted in the possession of this trait, saying (Tehillim 119:161), "Princes pursued me for naught and my heart feared at Your word." We find that the majestic, exalted angels constantly fear and tremble before Hashem's greatness. Chazal say by way of analogy (Chagigah 13b), "What is the source of the stream of fire?-the sweat of the holy creatures." The angels respond in this manner because of the fear of the Majesty of Hashem, which is constantly upon them and which causes them anxiety as to any possible failings on their part in relation to the honor and holiness demanded by His Presence. Whenever and wherever the Divine Presence manifests itself there is trembling, tumult and fright. As Scripture states (Tehillim 68:9), "The earth shook ; even the heavens dripped. .. before Hashem" and (Isaiah 63:19), "Is it for them that You tore the heavens, that You descended, that mountains flowed before You?" How much more so, then, should human beings tremble and quake in the knowledge that they stand always in the presence of Hashem and so might easily do what is not in accordance with the majestic honor of Hashem. As Eliphaz said to Job (Job 15:14,15), "What is man that he would be found pure? Would one born of woman be found righteous? He does not put trust in His holy ones and the heavens are not pure in His eyes" and (Ibid. 4:18,19), "He puts no trust in His servants and invests not His angels with light. Much more so dwellers m houses of clay . . . This should certainly cause every man to constantly fear and tremble. In the words of Elihu (Ibid. 37:1,2), "At this, too, my heart fears and is moved from its place, hearing the clamor of His voice..." This is the true fear which should always be upon the face of a Tzaddik and never depart from him.

There are two aspects to this type of fear - the first pertaining to the present or the future, and the second to the past. In relation to the present, a person should always fear and worry that there may be present in what he is doing, or that there might enter into what he is going to do, that which is not in accordance with the honor of Hashem, as mentioned above. In relation to the past, a person must fear and worry that he might unknowingly have committed some sin. Bava ben Buta, for example, (Kerithuth 25a) would sacrifice a provisional guilt offering every day.

And Job, after his sons' feast, "arose and sacrificed burntofferings according to the number of all of them; for Job said, `Perhaps my sons have sinned.. .' " (Job 1:5). Chazal commented along these lines in connection with the oil of anointment with which Moshe anointed Aaron, as he was commanded to do in the face of the interdict (Exodus 30:32), "Let it not anoint the flesh of man." They feared that they might have violated the interdict in some way and have committed an act of desecration. (Horioth 12a) : "Moshe worried, saying, `Perhaps I have desecrated the oil of anointment,' at which a heavenly voice went forth and said (Tehillim 133:2), 'As the good oil upon the head descends upon the beard, the beard of Aaron... as the dew of Hermon.' Just as there is no desecration in relation to the dew of Hermon, so, too, there is no desecration in relation to the oil of anointment upon the beard of Aaron.' But still Aaron was worried, `It may be that Moshe did not commit an act of desecration, but that I did,' at which a heavenly voice went forth and said, `How good and how pleasant for brothers to dwell together.' Just as Moshe is not guilty of desecration, you, too, are not guilty." We see, then, that it is characteristic of Tzaddikim to worry even in relation to the mitzvos that they have done, fearing that some trace of impurity might have intruded itself into them (Hashem forbid) . Abraham, after he had gone to the assistance of his nephew, Lot, who had been taken captive, was afraid that his actions had not been entirely pure. As Chazal said (Bereshith Rabbah 44.4) in relation to the verse (Bereishis 15:1), "Do not fear, Avram," "R. Levi said, `Because Abraham was afraid and said, `Perhaps among all the soldiers I have killed there was one righteous man or one who feared Heaven,' he was told, `Do not fear, Avram.' " And in Tana D'bei Eliyahu (Chapter 25) it is stated, "'Do not fear, Avram' - 'Do not fear' is said only to one who fears Heaven in truth." This is the true fear about which it was said (Berachoth 33b), "Hashem has in His world only a treasure of fear of Heaven." Only Moshe because of his intimacy with Hashem could attain it easily. Others, unquestionably, are greatly deterred by the earthy element within them. However, it befits every Tzaddik to exert himself to attain as much of this fear as he can, as The posuk states (Tehillim 34:10), "Let His holy ones fear Hashem."

CHAPTER XXV

THE MANNER OF ACQUIRING FEAR OF SIN

THE MANNER of acquiring this fear is to reflect upon two truths. The first is that the Divine Presence is found everywhere and Hashem looks to all things, great and small, nothing being hidden from His eyes, whether by its magnitude or by its smallness. Great and small, imposing and humble alike, He sees and understands without distinction. As stated in the Posuk (Isaiah 6:3), "The whole earth is filled with His glory" and (Jeremiah 23:24), "Do I not fill heaven and earth?" and (Tehillim 113:5), "Who is like Hashem, our Hashem, who sits on high, who stoops to look upon heaven and earth" and (Ibid. 138:6), "For G- d is high; He sees the lowly and knows the proud from afar." Once it has become clear to one that wherever he may be, he is standing before the Presence of Hashem, there will come to him of itself, the fear and trepidation of going astray in his actions so that they do not accord with the majesty of Hashem. As it is stated (Avos 2.1), "Know what is above you: a seeing eye, a listening ear and a book in which all of your deeds are inscribed." Since Hashem looks to everything, sees everything and knows everything, it follows that all actions leave an impression. And they are all inscribed in a book, whether they be in one's favor or against him. This understanding, however, imprints itself in a person's mind only through constant reflection and deep analysis, for since it is removed from our senses, our intelligence will formulate it only after much thought and consideration. And even after the idea has been assimilated, it may be easily lost if it is not constantly reflected upon. It is seen, then, that just as protracted thought is the means of acquiring ever-present fear, so is inattentiveness and desistence from thought its greatest deterrent, whether it results from preoccupation or is intentional. All inattentiveness nullifies constancy of fear. As Hashem commanded in relation to a king (Dvarim 17:19), "And it shall be with him and he shall read it all the days of his life so that he may learn to fear, Hashem." This teaches us that fear is learned only by uninterrupted study. It is to be noted that we have "so that he may learn to fear," rather than "so that he may fear," the underlying idea being that this fear is not naturally attainable, but that, to the contrary, it is far removed from one because of the physical nature of his senses and can be acquired only through learning. And the only manner in which one may learn to fear is through constant, uninterrupted study of the Torah and its ways, through constantly (when sitting, walking, retiring and arising) reflecting upon and analyzing, until it implants itself in his mind, the truth of the existence of Hashem's Presence in all places, and of our literally standing before Him at all periods and times. He will then fear Hashem in truth. This was the intent of David's prayer (Tehillim 86:11), "Teach me, O Hashem, Your ways 1 will walk in Your truth. Unite my heart to fear Your Name."

CHAPTER XXVI

CONCERNING THE TRAIT OF HOLINESS

HOLINESS IS TWO-FOLD. Its beginning is labor and its end reward; its beginning, exertion and its end, a gift. That is, it begins with one's sanctifying himself and ends with his being sanctified. As Chazal have said (Yoma 39a), "If one sanctifies himself a little, he is sanctified a great deal; if he sanctifies himself below, he is sanctified from above." Exertion in this respect consists in one's completely separating and removing himself from earthiness and clinging always, at all periods and times, to his Hashem. It was because of the possession of this trait that the Prophets were called "angels," as stated in relation to Aaron (Malachi 2:7), "For the lips of the Priest will guard knowledge, and Torah will be sought from his mouth for he is an angel of Hashem of Hosts." And (II Chronicles 36:16), "And they disparaged the angels of G -d.. . " Even when one is engaged in the physical activities required by his body, his soul must not deviate from its elevated intimacy, as it is stated (Tehillim 63:9), "My soul clings to You; Your right arm sustains me ."However, because it is beyond a person's ability to place himself in this situation, since, in the last analysis, he is a creature of flesh and blood, I have stated that the end of Holiness is a gift. What one can do is to persevere in the pursuit of true understanding and constantly give thought to the sanctification of deeds.

In the end, Hashem leads him upon the path that he desires to follow, causes His Holiness to rest upon him, and sanctifies him, thus enabling him to keep a constant intimacy with Him, Hashem. Where his nature hinders him, Hashem will aid and assist him, as it is stated (Tehillim 84:12), "He does not withhold good from those who walk in purity."

This is the intent of the above statement. "If one sanctifies himself a little," by what he can acquire through his own exertions, "he is sanctified a great deal," by the help he receives from Hashem.

If one sanctifies himself with the Holiness of his Creator, even his physical actions come to Holiness. This is illustrated by the eating of sacrificial offerings (itself a mitzvah) in relation to which Chazal have said (Pesachim 59b), "The Priests eat and the owners are atoned for."

Note the distinction between one who is Pure and one who is Holy. The earthy actions of the first are necessary ones, and he is motivated by necessity alone, so that his actions escape the evil in earthiness and remain pure. But they do not approach Holiness, for it were better if one could get along without them. One who is Holy, however, and clings constantly to his Hashem, his soul traveling in channels of truth, amidst the love and fear of his Creator -such a person is as one walking before Hashem in the Land of the Living, here in this world. Such a person is himself considered a tabernacle, a sanctuary, an altar. As Chazal have said (Bereshith Rabbah 47.8), " `And Hashem went up from him' (Bereishis 35:13) -the patriarchs are the Divine chariot" and, "The righteous are the Divine chariot." The Divine Presence dwells with the Holy as it dwelt in the Temple. It follows, then, that the food which they eat is as a sacrifice offered upon the fire. There is no question that what was brought up upon the altar was greatly elevated because of its being sacrificed before the Divine Presence, elevated to such an extent that its entire species throughout the world was blessed, as Chazal indicate in the Midrash (Tanchumah Tetzaveh). In the same way, the food and drink of the Holy man is elevated and is considered as if it had actually been sacrificed upon the altar. As our Sages 'of blessed memory have said (Kethuvoth 105b), "If one brings a gift to a Scholar, it is as if he offers up first fruit" and (Yoma 71a), "In the place of libation, let him fill the throat of the Scholars with wine." The meaning here is not that Scholars should lust, glutton-like, to fill their throats with food and drink (Hashem forbid), but rather, as we have indicated, that Scholars, who are Holy in their ways and in all of their deeds, are literally comparable to the sanctuary and the altar, for the Divine Presence dwells with them just as it dwelled in the sanctuary. Their consuming of food is similar to the offering up of a sacrifice upon the altar, and the filling of their throats is analogous to the filling of the basins. In accordance with this view, anything at all which is made use of by them in some way is elevated and enhanced through having been employed by a righteous individual, by one who communes with the Holiness of Hashem. Chazal have already referred to "the stones of the place" that Jacob took and set around his head (Chullin 91b), "R. Yitzchak said, `This teaches us that they all gathered together, each one saying, `Let the righteous one lay his head upon me.'"

In fine, Holiness consists in one's clinging so closely to his G -d that in any deed he might perform he does not depart or move from Hashem, until the physical objects of which he makes use become more elevated because of his having used them, than he descends from his communion and from his high plane because of his having occupied himself with them. This obtains, however, only in relation to one whose mind and intelligence cling so closely to the greatness, majesty and Holiness of Hashem that it is as if he is united with the celestial angels while yet in this world. I have already indicated that one cannot accomplish this by himself, but must awaken himself to it and strive for it. But first, he must have attained all of the noble traits previously mentioned - from the beginning of Watchfulness until the Fear of Sin. Only in this way will he arrive at Holiness and succeed in it; for if he lacks the preceding traits, he is akin to an outsider, the bearer of an imperfection, about whom it is said (Numbers 18:4), "An outsider shall not come near." But if, after having undergone all these preparations, he steadfastly pursues with strong love and great fear, the contemplation of the greatness of Hashem and the might of His majesty, he will separate himself little by little from earthy considerations and in all his actions and movements will direct his heart to the intimacies of true communion until there is conferred upon him a spirit from on high and Hashem causes His Name to dwell with him as He does with all of His Holy ones. He will then be in actuality like an angel of Hashem, and all of his actions, even the lowly, physical ones, will be accounted as sacrifices and Divine service.

It is to be seen that the means of acquiring this trait arc much separation, intense contemplation of the secrets of Divine governance and the mysteries of creation, and understanding of the majesty of Hashem and His excellence, to the point where one cleaves closely to Him and is capable of performing physical activities with the same motivation with which it befits the Priest to slaughter the sacrificial animal, receive its blood, and sprinkle it in order to receive from Hashem the blessing of life and peace. Without the above orientation one will find it impossible to attain Holiness, and regardless of what level he may have reached, he will nonetheless remain earthy and physical, like all other men.

What assists one toward the acquisition of this trait is much solitude and separation, which, by eliminating the claims upon a person, allows his soul to grow in strength and to unite itself with the Creator.

The deterrents to Holiness are a lack of true understanding and much association with people; for earthiness finds its counterpart and takes on new strength, and the soul remains trapped within it, unable to escape. However, when one dissociates himself from them and remains alone, preparing himself for the reception of His Holiness, he is conducted along the path which he wishes to travel; and, with the help that Hashem gives him, his soul grows strong within him, overcomes his physical element, unites itself with the Holiness of Hashem and perfects itself in it. From this level one proceeds to an even higher one, that of The Holy Spirit, his understanding coming to transcend the bounds of human nature. It is possible for one to reach such a high degree of communion with G-d as to be given the key to the revival of the dead, as it was given to Elijah and Elisha. It is this gift which reveals the strength of one's union with Hashem, for since He is the source of life, the giver of life to all living creatures, as Chazal have said (Taanis 2a), "Three keys were not entrusted to intermediaries: the key of the revival of the dead." -since this is so, then one who is perfectly united with Hashem will be able to draw even life from Him; for it is that which more than anything else is particularly attributed to Him, as I have written. Hence the conclusion of the Baraitha: " Holiness leads to the Holy Spirit, and the Holy Spirit leads to the Revival of the Dead."

And now, dear reader, I realize that you know that I have not exhausted in this work all of the provisions of Saintliness and that I have not said all there is to say about it, for it has no end, and there is no conclusion to thought. However, I have said a little about each of the particulars of the Baraitha upon which this work is based. This may be a beginning toward a broader study of these views, in that their nature has been revealed and their paths exposed so that one may walk steadily upon them. In relation to all such things it has been said (Mishlei 1:5), "The sage will listen and add to his wisdom and the man of understanding will acquire devices" and, "One who seeks purification is assisted therein" (Shabbath 104a). "For Hashem gives wisdom; from His mouth stem knowledge and understanding" (Mishlei 2:6) wherewith every man may set his path aright before Hashem.

It is understood that each individual must guide and direct himself according to his calling and according to the particular activities in which he is engaged. The path of Saintliness appropriate to one whose Torah is his calling is unsuited to one who must hire himself out to work for his neighbor, and the path of neither of these is suitable for one who is engaged in business. This holds true for all of the particulars in the affairs of men, each calling for a path of Saintliness corresponding to its nature. This is not to say that Saintliness varies in nature. It is unquestionably the same for everyone, in that its intent is the doing of that which brings pleasure to the Creator. But in view of the fact that circumstances vary, it follows that the means by which they are to be directed toward the desired goal vary in kind. One who, out of necessity, plies a humble trade, can be a true Saint, just as one from whose mouth learning never departs. It is written (Mishlei 16:4), "Hashem created everything for His sake" and (Ibid. 3:6), "In all your ways know Him and He will straighten your paths."

May Hashem in His mercy open our eyes to His Torah, teach us His ways, and lead us in His paths; and may we be worthy of honoring His name and bringing pleasure to Him.

"The honor of Hashem will endure forever; Hashem will be happy in His works" (Tehillim 104:31). "Let Israel be happy in its Maker, the sons of Zion rejoice in their King" (Ibid. 149:2).

Made in the USA
Columbia, SC
21 January 2020